DISTANCE EDUCATION

DISTANCE EDUCATION

Student Support Services

V.P. Matheswaran

ANMOL PUBLICATIONS PVT. LTD.
NEW DELHI - 110 002 (INDIA)

ANMOL PUBLICATIONS PVT. LTD.
4374/4B, Ansari Road, Daryaganj
New Delhi - 110 002
Ph.: 23261597, 23278000
Visit us at: www.anmolpublications.com

Distance Education: Student Support Services

First Published, 2005

ISBN 81-261-2469-5

PRINTED IN INDIA

Published by J.L. Kumar for Anmol Publications Pvt. Ltd., New Delhi - 110 002 and Printed at Mehra Offset Press, Delhi.

Contents

Foreword

"Distance Education" has expanded to a large extent during the last four decades and due to this expansion, distance education is now considered as a separate discipline. The growth of U.K. Open University has contributed extensively for the expansion of distance education world over. In India, the National Open University, viz., Indira Gandhi National Open University (IGNOU) during the last two decades of its existence has expanded considerably and is providing quality distance education to several lakhs of aspirants of higher education. Similarly several States in India including Tamil Nadu have established separate Open Universities at the State level and these State Open Universities are complementing the efforts of the National Open University in their respective states. The establishment and growth of the National Open University and State Open Universities in India apart from bringing higher education to the doorsteps of the aspirants of higher education contribute immensely for the growth of this new discipline—Distance Education. Fairly good number of books and journals are available authored by Distance Educationists from U.K., USA and other advanced countries; but the publications by Indian writers in this field is very much limited. Publication of books and journals not only help the growth of this new discipline but also help dissemination of information to the people working in this field. In this context, I appreciate the efforts of Dr. V.P. Matheswaran, Faculty of the Department of Adult and Continuing Education, University of Madras in bringing out this publication on "Distance Education: Student Support Services". This book provides fairly good coverage on distance education and the role of student support services in distance education. It is a fact that student support services play a predominant role in distance education and the success of distance education programmes largely depends on the student support services made available to the distance learners. I congratulate Dr. Matheswaran, for his contribution to distance education in this book and wish him success in all his future endeavors.

—Prof. M.S. Palanichamy
Vice-Chancellor
Tamil Nadu Open University
Chennai

Preface

Education is one of the tools for making people as good citizens. Distance education is an alternative system for formal education. Non-formal and distance education fulfils the democratic aspirations of people and a right step in spreading for achieving the goals of 'Education for All'. U.K. Open University at the international level, Indira Gandhi Open University at the national level and Ten State Open Universities have contributed immensely for the development of distance education. This book deals with non-formal adult education, distance education, open learning, online/virtual education, level of utilization of the support services and learners attitude towards open university systems. This book will be very useful to the distance educators and research scholars who pursue research studies in open/distance education.

I offer my sincere and grateful thanks to Professor Dr. R. Jayagopal and Professor (Mrs.) Rajkumari Chandrasekar former heads of the department of Adult and Continuing Education, University of Madras for their guidance and continued encouragement. I am grateful to Mr. P.V. Ramalinggam, P.R.O., University of Madras for his encouragement and continued support.

I am greatly indebted to my beloved parents for their blessings. I would like to thank my wife Dr. A. Parmeswari, Faculty of Chemistry, Government Arts College, and my daughter M. Kural Vaani for showing interest in all my endeavors. Also, I thank Mr. C. Pillai TNBH for his efforts in bringing this publication,

I am thankful to Anmol Publications Pvt. Ltd., New Delhi for publishing this book.

V.P. Matheswaran

List of Tables

List of Charts

Abbreviations

A.U.	Athabasca University
A.I.O.U.	Allama Iqbal Open University
B.D.P.	Bachelor's Degree Programme
B.R.A.O.U.	Dr.B.R. Ambedkar Open University
C.C.I.	Correspondence Course Institute
C.C.T.U.	Central China Television University
C.O.L.	Commonwealth of Learning
D.E.	Distance Education
D.E.C.	Distance Education Council
I.C.C.E.	International Council for Correspondence Education
I.C.D.E.	International Council for Distance Education
I.G.N.O.U.	Indira Gandhi National Open University
O.L.S.	Open Learning System
O.U.	Open University
O.U.S.	Open University System
P.G.	Post Graduate
U.G.	Under Graduate
R.C.	Regional Centre
S.C.	Study Centre

S.T.R.I.D.E.	Staff Training and Research Institute for Distance Education
T.N.O.U.	Tamil Nadu Open University
U.G.C.	University Grants Commission
U.K.O.U.	United Kingdom Open University
Y.C.M.O.U.	Yaswantrao Chavan Maharastra Open University

1

Alternative for Conventional Education System

Education is a unique investment in the present day world. Education develops manpower for different levels of economy. It constitutes the core of human resource development. The growth and development of educational facilities of all kinds in the third world countries with plans to induct all sectors of community is interesting and instructive. Financial constraints and poverty are the rudimentary factors responsible for haphazard growth and development of educational system in these countries. India is no exception to this phenomenon if we look at the educational scene in our country. During the last five decades, certain trends are clearly visible and among other educational developments the need for distance education is highly emphasized. Tertiary level education at a distance is not necessarily the exclusive domain of adults. At times it is taken for granted that distance education is synonymous with adult education. This is the second chance education for the adults, who have missed their earlier opportunity for attending a conventional university education in their youth.

Why need Alternative Education?

India is home for 17 per cent of the world's total population comprising one billion of different socio-economic and cultural backgrounds. The formal system of higher education is accessible only to a fraction of the masses. The programmes of study offered by various universities fulfill limited requirements of particular regions and segments of the society and people have to approach different universities offering courses of their choice. Weaker sections of the society find it difficult to receive education of their choice in nearby institutions at affordable costs. The National Policy on Education (1986) recognizes that educational opportunities in India are both inadequate and in equal. It emphasizes that a cost-effective alternative to the present conventional system of higher education can be seen in distance education and that open universities can provide higher educational opportunities to those who have been deprived of it due to one or another reason. The modular structure and flexible delivery system makes distance education programme ideal to meet the desired higher educational needs of a wide class of learners.

University of Delhi is the first in India to launch distance education in 1962 in the name of correspondence courses. In 1961, the Central Advisory Board of Education appointed a committee to recommend on the nature, scope and mode for the organization of correspondence courses in Indian Universities. The first state Open University was set up in 1982 in Andhra Pradesh, now known as Dr. B.R. Ambedkar Open University. The first national Open University, known as the Indira Gandhi National Open University, was set up in 1985 by an act of parliament.

At present, there are about 104 directorates/centres for distance education in various universities, 10 state open universities and a national Open University. The growth rate (16.2%) of distance education has been particularly higher than that (3.9%) of the formal system. The tenth plan document of the Government of India has projected that by the end of the plan period, the share of open and distance learners might increase to 30-40%. Open/Distance education has emerged, as a viable and an effective option to a large section of youth having no access to the conventional universities.

Non-Formal/Non-Conventional Education

The educational policy of India (1986), while highlighting the objectives of its new package of educational reforms, emphasized the need for ensuring "equality of educational opportunities". One of the main packages includes the expansion of non-formal and non-conventional education. According to the constitution, India was committed to provide within ten years from the commencement of the constitution, free and compulsory education to boys and girls up to the age of 14. Even now this goal has not been achieved. According to the Ramamurthy Committee (1990) Report, 41.9 per cent of the boys and 61.5 per cent of the girls in the age group of 6-14 do not attend the schools. If the Constitutional commitment is to be honoured, distance education is the only answer, which will suck into its vortex all those left outs, push outs and new starters.

Since 1991 India has witnessed tremendous resurgence in the realm of economic activity, due to restructuration, liberalization and privatization of public sector undertakings. A market economy is thus visible. If this is the reality, it is evident that the private, public and joint sector corporate and service institutions need millions of the skill oriented human resources with new outlook. The existing higher educational opportunities are quite inadequate to cope with the economic mutation. Access to these institutions is still a challenging proposition for millions of young adults who have aspirations but are unable to complete the cycle of the higher education. In this twilight zone, as it is apparent, distance education is the only answer and is the only instrument which can provide education, training and skill at the doorsteps of the learners.

Non-formal education is not entirely new. Correspondence education is added as another dimension to the facilities of education starting from school to tertiary level. It is known as home study or postal tuition, which is popular by called as distance learning or distance education. All these concepts more or less mean the same system and it is found as an effective alternative to the present formal education. Distance education carries certain characteristics of non-formal education in its flexibility and student oriented schedule. Table 1.1 shows the differences between conventional and distance education systems.

TABLE 1.1

Conventional Vs Distance Education

Conventional Education	*Distance Education*
Learners meet regularly	Learners may be separated by time or space
Learners meet with an instructor regularly	Learners rarely if ever meet face to face with the instructor
Materials are used as directed by an instructor	Learning materials need to be self explanatory
Instructors need to be at the instruction where the course takes place	Instructors can physically be anywhere
Instructors tend to be from one institution or travel to it for the course	Instructors from a range of instructions can take part in the course

Continuing Education

Life-long learning activities presented in policy statements are usually focused not on the aspects of the contribution to the economy or human resource development but on the aspects of the mental satisfaction of people. In modern developing societies the concept of education as a life long process or continuing education derives its validity from the fact that the present day society is not based on static conditions but subject to rapid and dynamic changes in all walks of life. The frontiers of knowledge are constantly expanding. Science and technology are taking rapid strides. The concept of continuing education is gaining popularity, particularly as a education in Indian universities. If the universities accept the responsibilities of improving skills of the vast human resources, they would render invaluable service to the community and meet urgently the felt human resource needs of national development. The condition in economic, political and social life are also changing rapidly with new inventions and adoption of new technology in the modes of media, communication and travel.

Global Perspective of Distance Education

In order to gain more insight into the delivery systems facilitating several types of education such as formal, non-formal, informal and lifelong education it is worthwhile to examine the global perspective of distance education which is one of the ubiquitous approaches followed currently. The origin of distance education can be traced to correspondence education, which has been in existence for over 100 years and still remains the most prevalent form of distance education. "Correspondence implies that two or more parties are in contact with one another in writing. Consequently, correspondence teaching is taken to mean teaching in writing, in the course of which the learner and teacher regularly write to each other". The educational transaction is facilitated by the print medium and the mail system. The modern history of correspondence education is traced back to 1840 when Issac Pitman offered shorthand courses through correspondence. The formal correspondence programs were initiated in Europe and USA in the later half of the 19th century. There were more than 200 correspondence schools in the United States by 1910 (Young, 1984).

The growth of correspondence education is due to the introduction of postage stamp and by 1930s the telephone was being used for instruction. In Russia, later in Australia and New Zealand, correspondence education was used extensively. In England, a number of private correspondence colleges were established. The widespread acceptance of correspondence mode of education generated interest in finding a more suitable term for the system encompassing a broader perspective. Non-formal education through multimedia had become part of the development and extension effort of most countries. An international forum the International Council for Correspondence Education (ICCE) was formed in 1938 with the pioneering efforts of J.N. Gibson and the first world conference of the Council was organized in 1938 at Victoria B.C. with 88 participants from Canada, Australia, USA, New Zealand and Scotland. Region and countrywise distribution of distance education institutes is given in Table 1.2.

TABLE 1.2

Region and Country-wise Distribution of Distance Education Institutes

Sl.No.	*Continents/Board Regions*	*Number of Countries*	*Number of Institutes*
1.	Africa	34	103
2.	Asia	13	90
3.	Australia	4	80
4.	Middle East	2	2
5.	Europe	17	170
6.	North America	2	194
7.	Caribbean	4	7
8.	Latin America	13	58
	Total	**89**	**704**

Source: UK Open University ICDL CD Rom Data Base, 1993.

The concept of distance education is used to denote a wide range of learning strategies, referred differently in different countries such as:

- Correspondence education (Most of the countries including India)
- Home Study (North America and Europe)
- Independent Study (North America)
- External Studies
- Open Learning
- Open University
- Off-Campus studies (Australia)
- Extra-Mural (New Zealand)
- Education a distance (Spanish Speaking Countries)
- Tele-Enalignment (France)
- Fern. Universitat (Germany)

All these denote the correspondence education only.

Commonwealth of Learning (COL)

An important landmark on the development of distance education in the Commonwealth countries has been the establishment of Commonwealth of Learning (COL) in 1988 at Vancouver in Canada at the instance of Commonwealth Ministers of Education and Commonwealth Heads of Government. It has contributed considerably in popularizing the distance education system and is also emphasizing the improvement of the quality of course materials, staff development and training and dual mode—a part of the course to be covered by face-to-face teaching and the rest through the distance mode. During the XV World Conference of the ICDE held in Bangkok in November, 1992, the presidents of ICDE and the Commonwealth of Learning signed an agreement to act jointly so as to encourage and facilitate research in distance education.

Distance Education—An Indian Scenario

Higher education in post-independent India has been wrought with dichotomies in its growth and development, quality vs quantity, elitism vs equal opportunities, selective vs open and formal, to name only a few. There has been an unprecedented growth of institutions of higher learning. While in 1951, there were 695 colleges and 22 universities only in 1993, the number of colleges and universities went up to 7720 and 210 respectively. The vast expansion without consideration of factors such as resources etc., the casualty has been the quality.

The Constitution of India provides for equal educational opportunities for all. At the same time, higher education has got to be selective to provide opportunities on the basis of certain of selection because of the scarce resources at its disposal. Many highly motivated could not go for higher education mainly due to reasons other than academic i.e., social, economic and environmental compulsions. There are about 94 percent of the relevant age group who are outside the system at the tertiary level. The term distance education encompasses the traditional, formal system of education and is characterized by flexibility and context, mode, media, materials and evaluation of learning, flexibility in admission requirements, choice of course, duration of programmes, and means of communication, etc.

Distance education at the tertiary level was introduced in India for the first time in 1962 by the University of Delhi. During 1963, an expert committee appointed by the University Grants Commission (UGC) with Prof. D.S. Kothari as Chairman recommended establishment of directorates of correspondence courses in universities. During 1960s only four institutes of correspondence education were in existence imparting under graduate courses only. During 1970-80, 21 universities established institutes of correspondence education. In 1994, 46 universities started instructions at all levels. In 1977-78, the enrolment in correspondence education (undergraduate and postgraduate levels) had gone up to 2.51 per cent and 11.92 percent respectively of the total enrolment. In the first five years, from 1971-72, the total enrolment of learners in correspondence courses revealed an annual growth rate of 9.7 per cent which went up to 15.2 per cent during 1975-76 to 1982-83. This led to the upgradation of the institute/directorates of correspondence courses which have been working as extension departments of the conventional universities. Most of the Correspondence Course Institutes (CCI) are importing education only through the print medium and issuing the conventional degrees. The UGC is working in this direction and has, after deliberations, circulated a detailed document to all the universities having correspondence courses Directorate/Departments, highlighting the reforms that are to be brought about for upgrading the CCIs to the distance mode.

A significant landmark in the history of distance education in India has been the launching of Satellite Television Experiments (SITE) in 1975 uniting 2330 villages of the economically backward states. Doordarshan's Education Television (ETV) Programmes comprising school television (STV), higher education television (HETV), UGC's countrywide class room.

Open Learning

Open Learning is learning without the usual restrictions and constraints normally associated with the traditional (class room) education. "Open Learning is an imprecise phrase to which a range of meanings can be, and is, attached. It eludes definition, but as an inscription to be carried in procession on a banner, gathering adherence and enthusiasms, it has great potential. For its very imprecision it enables to accommodate any different ideas and aims and the two terms of the phrase carry with them emotional overtones..." Open Learning Systems are described as systems which are designed to offer opportunities for part-time study, for learning at a distance and for innovations in the curriculum. They are intended to allow access to wider sectarian of adult population, to enable learners to compensate for lost opportunities in the past or to acquire new skills and qualifications required for future career development. Open Learning System aims to redress social or educational inequality and offer opportunities that were not provided by conventional colleges or universities.

Open University

Open universities are institutions, which provide non-traditional innovative type of education irrespective of age, caste, creed, sex differences and without bringing the clientele to its portals. It uses all the possible means of communication and the postal system being one of them.

The establishment of United Kingdom Open University (UKOU) in 1969 acted as a catalyst for the provision of higher education 'through multimedia system that harnessed educational broadcasting to correspondence teaching and other methods' (Perry 1977) and it was both continuing a century-old tradition of correspondence education, and raising the methods of independent study to a new level of sophistication by integrating the electronic media with its print-led courses (Daniel 1977). The establishment of Open University was a landmark in the history of distance education and the period after that has been the most progressive period.

In 1982, during the 12th conference held at Vancouver, the International Council of Correspondence Education (ICCE) was renamed as the International Council of Distance

Education (ICDE). Promotion and Development of Research and Scholarship on Distance Education was included as an objective of the ICDE. An important objective of ICDE is to offer its member institutions collaborative mechanism at global and regional levels, through which they can cooperate to improve their own positions and performance and in order to make advocacy and lobbying functions more forceful and efficient.

India has today one national open university namely Indira Gandhi National Open University (1985) and ten state open universities. They are Dr. B.R. Ambedkar Open University, Hyderabad (1982), Kota Open University, Rajasthan (1987), Nalanda Open University, Bihar (1987), Vardhaman Mahaveer Open University (1987), Yashwantrao Chavan Maharashtra Open University (1989), Raja Bhoj Open University, Madhya Pradesh (1991), Dr. Baba Saheb Ambedkar Open University, Gujarat (1994), Karnataka State Open Universities (1996), Netaji Subhash Open Universities (1997), U.P. Rajashri Tandon Open Universities (1998) and Tamil Nadu Open University (2002). Eighty six dual mode traditional universities are offering distance education programmes. During the last 2 years alone, 36 new universities/institutes have introduced open and distance learning systems. Table 1.3 shows the year-wise enrolment of learners in the ten state open universities.

Distance Education Council

Distance Education Council (DEC), a statutory body under the IGNOU Act has been established, on the recommendation of the UGC in 1992, to operationalize the functions assigned to the IGNOU. The Distance Education Council is an apex body of distance education in India. The Vision and Mission of the Distance Education Council is are as follows:

TABLE 1.3

Year-wise Enrolment of Ten State Open Universities

Sl.No.	*Open Universities*	*1999*	*2000*	*2001*	*2002*	*2003*
01.	Dr. B.R. Ambedkar Open University	63000	99082	89938	90492	125225
02.	Nalantha Open University	—	—	—	2,110	4,395
03.	Yashwantra Chavan Maharashtra Open University	110700	104551	113500	113756	110683
04.	Vardhaman Mahaveer Open University	—	2862	9325	10973	3557
05.	Raja Bhoj Open University	—	51422	63919	104116	137326
06.	Dr. Baba Saheb Ambedkar Open University	—	9878	11247	8565	1260
07.	Karnataka State Open Universities	—	—	37037	35659	31666
08.	U.P. Rajashri Tandon Open Universities	—	—	1089	2999	—
09.	Netaji Subhas Open Unversities	—	1459	1967	2752	4210
10.	Tamil Nadu Open University	—	—	—	—	—

Vision of Distance Education Council will promote the culture of lifelong learning for every one, everywhere and any time. The application of ICTs and multimedia approaches will be encouraged for improving access, equity and effectiveness of learning. The strategy of promotion of ODL will focus on creation of an enlightened and prosperous society. Mission of Distance Education Council will strive for coordinated development of open and distance learning system and ensure maintenance of standards in education. The council will accordingly formulate policies and make concerted efforts to plan and guide distance education activities for equalization of educational opportunities, which in effect will widen the base of human capital formation through open and distance education.

Functions of the Distance Education Council

I. It shall be the general duty of the Distance Education Council to take all such steps as are consistent with the provisions of the Act, the statutes and the ordinance for the promotion of the open university/distance education systems, its coordinated development, and the determination of its standards, and in particular:

1. To develop a network of open university/distance education institutions in the country in consultation with the state governments, Universities and other concerned agencies.
2. To identify priority areas in which distance education programmes should be organized and to provide such support as may be considered necessary for organizing such programmes.
3. To identify the specific client groups and the types of the progerammes to be organized for them, and to promote and encourage the organization of such programmes through the network of open universities/distance education institutions.
4. To promote an innovative system of university level of education, flexible and open, in regard to methods and pace of learning, combination of courses, eligibility for enrolment, age of entry, conduct of examination and organize various courses and programmes.
5. To promote the organization of programmes of human resource development for open university/ distance education system.

6. To initiate and organize measures for joint development of courses and programmes and research in distance education technologies and practices.
7. To recommend to the Board of Management the pattern and nature of financial assistance that may be sanctioned to open universities/distance education institutions and the conditions that may have to be fulfilled by them to receive such assistance.
8. To take such steps are necessary to ensure the coordinated development of the open university/distance education system in the country.
9. To establish and develop arrangements for coordinating and sharing the instructional materials prepared by different open universities/distance education institutions and the student support systems with a view to avoiding duplication of efforts.
10. To evolve procedures for sharing of courses and programmes and for the payment of royalty or other charges to the members of the network whose courses and programmes are used by other members.
11. To prescribe broad norms for charging fees from learners who join various programmes offered by the network of open universities/distance education institutions.
12. To collect, compile and disseminate information relating to the courses and programmes offered by various open universities/distance education institutions.
13. To avoid State Government, Universities and other

concerned agencies on their proposals to set up open universities, or to introduce programmes of distance education.

14. To appoint review committees from time to time to study and assess the performance of the open universities/distance education institutions participating in the network on any aspect relevant to the functioning of the network.
15. To prescribe a board framework for courses and programmes including the pattern and structure.
16. To evolve norms, procedures and practices in respect of admission, evaluation, completion of courses requirements, transfer of credits, etc., of learners admitted to the programmes of the open university/distance education network and for the award of certificates, diplomas and degrees to them.
17. To evolve guidelines for the organization of learners support services for the open university/ distance education programmes.
18. To take such measures as are necessary, consistent, with the objects of the university to provide innovative, flexible and open system of university education for the promotion, including introduce and continuation of courses and programmes which confirm to the standards prescribed by DEC, to maintain such standards in the institutions offering distance education programmes and prevent, through such measures are as considered appropriate, institutions form offering courses, programmes which do not conform to the standards laid down by the council.
19. To appoint committees for advising and assisting

the DEC in the performance of any of its function or exercise of any of its powers.

II. The Distance Education Council shall:

1. Appoint committees, which shall assess, in consultation with the concerned open universities/ distance education institutions, the development grants required by them for a five years period and only recommendations to the Board of Management.
2. Sanction grants to open universities/distance education institutions for specific projects on the basis of reports by duly appointed committees and in accordance with guidelines prescribed for the purpose and report such approvals to the Board of Management.

III. Financial assistance under clause (4) (b) may be sanctioned only to the following categories of institutions.

1. An open university established by or under an Act of a state Legislature and declared fit to recall assistance from central sources under section 12-B of the UGC Act.
2. Any other university as defined in section 2(f) of the IGC Act provided that such a university is declared fit, wherever applicable, under section 12-B of that Act.
3. An institution deemed to be a university under section 3 of the UGC Act.

Online Education

The Internet and web technologies replace the traditional institutional boundaries to expertise and knowledge. Cyber age has an immense impact on the life style of the people.

The world has become like a "Small Village" with the expansion of the information technology and cyber revolution. The Internet gives everyone who seeks information access to resources once held within the ivory tower. Learners can talk with experts from elite institutions by accessing their web sites. Learners can enter libraries, discuss with Professors worldwide. These challenges to traditional systems of learning have given us the opportunity to rethink how knowledge is acquired and how to design on-line education for the adult learners.

Information Technology in Distance Education

Developments in the field of information technology, and expansion of infrastructure for communication all over the country have created an unprecedented opportunity to serve the needs of continuing education and to meet the demands for equal opportunities for higher education. Now-a-days, audio/video conferencing, synchronized presentation tools, digital libraries, internet programmed languages, inter personal communication tools and authoring tools are common and can be used for imparting knowledge in the distance education systems. The chart 1.1 shows the communication aspects in distance education.

At present, there are 311 universities/institutions in the country (19 central university, 206 state universities, 86 deemed to be universities) 13 Institute of National importance and 5 Institutions established under State Legislative Act. Government of India spends 4 per cent of the total gross national income on education. Of this 4 per cent, less than 1 per cent is spend for higher education. Alternatively, universities can offer need based education, training and extension programmes with quality consciousness through distance/open mode as this requires smaller investment as compared to the conventional mode.

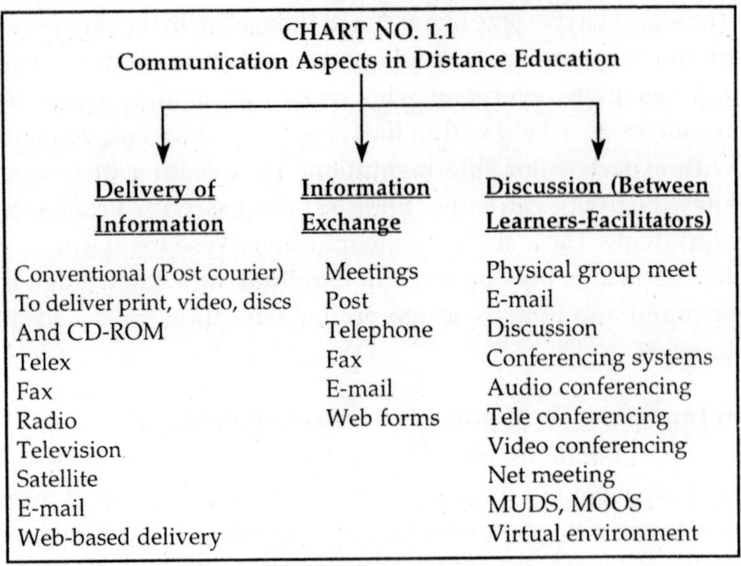

CHART NO. 1.1
Communication Aspects in Distance Education

Computer Assisted Instruction

The history of computer assisted instruction, first attempted using time sharing computers during 1960s, is clearly described by Harasim and her colleagues (Harasim, Hiltz, Teles and Turoff, 1995). Communication took place over dumb terminals connected to mainframe computers or dial-up telephone lines. In 1969, the U.S. government experimented with dedicated telephone lines data exchange by constructing the ARPANET (Advanced Research Project Agency Network) to contact researchers with remote computer centres to share messages. The electronic mail (e-mail) function was born and became immensely popular. Other communication network (e.g., USENET, BITNET, CSNET) followed are still predominantly connecting researches and scientists.

Murray Turoff is given credit for designing the first computer conferencing system in 1970 (Hiltz and Turoff, 1993). Today there are many conferencing systems available that support not only the discussion feature but also other more sophisticated features including personal messaging and audio and video capability. Computer conferencing systems were applied to course activity in higher education during the 1980s and remain a prominent feature of on-line education today.

Distance Education Vs Online Education

According to the U.S. congress for technology assessment, distance education refers to "linking of a teacher and Learners in several geographic locations via technology that allows for interaction" (Daniel & Stevens, 1998). Many distance education institutions that have come to adopt a strong online presence were functioning prior to the Internet by relying on individually directed study, mail, the telephone, and/or infrequent residential sessions for contact between learners and institutions. For example, United kingdom's Open University, which initiated use of computer conferencing as a small adjunct to a large multimedia course (Harasim et.al., 1995). Fielding, as is true for a few other academic institutions such as the Union Graduate school, Empire state college, and the University without wall, established a distance education model many years ago. This purpose is to provide an educational opportunity for a group of geographically dispersed, adult, mid-career professionals who could not easily give up their family and work responsibilities to move to a campus based institutions for a lengthy period of time. Table 1.4. shows the comparison of distance education and on-line education.

Adult Learner

Education institutions are trying to reach out its clientele as never before. Most current online students are professionals looking for additional training (Green, 2000). Continuing education is the fastest growth area within the educational plane. The term life-long learning has become a catchphrase

TABLE 1.4

Comparison of Distance Education and Online Education

Distance Education	*Online Education*
Little or no contact between learners	Learners can freely interact
Group discussion only possible through physical meetings.	Group discussion possible through video/tele-conferencing
Lacks competition and encouragement on the course	Competition and encouragement between learners is achieved
Complete feeling of isolation	To some extent ignores feeling of isolation
Cheaper with more students enroll but high fixed costs	Costs higher with more intake of students but low fixed costs
Very rare to involve more than one institute.	Can be consortium of institutes and brings expertise from different areas

to indicate the need, and wish, for ongoing personal growth and academic learning. Adult participation in learning is usually voluntary and is often stimulated by life transitions and changes where education can offer a resolution. More adults have multiple commitments to family, work, and friends. This means that the opportunity to complete courses and training over the Internet can be a god sent, enabling them to retain those commitments and work around the built in flexibility of the electronic environment. The qualities of education that seem to accommodate the developmental needs of adult learners may be well captured by the online learning environment.

Development of On-line Education

The demand for on-line education comes from the need for life-long learning and the need to continue professional and work-related training. Most universities and training institutions in United Kingdom use computer networks as an adjunct to more traditional classroom experiences. Some assignments and occasional face-to-face course might be offered online to take advantage of the medium's flexibility regarding time and place. Athabasca university which began as a correspondence programme in Canada in 1972 now offers many on-line graduate programmes (www.athabasca.ca). Most of the distance education institutions directly entered in the on-line education. The private educational institutions are selling the courses through Internet. Many corporations have corporate universities with on-line components. The corporate university provides information for corporate university organizers that includes a newsletter, e-news, and an annual conference.

Roberts and Jones (2000) models of on-line teaching

1. The naive model, which relies on posting lecture notes on the World Wide Web with no opportunities for interaction.
2. The standard model, which draws on the web technology to encourage interaction among learners and faculties about the course.
3. The evolutionary model, which allows the methods of course delivery throughout the term.
4. The radical model, which dispenses with lectures and relies on interactive groups of learners.

The Online Systems

A University of Illinois Report 1999 defines online instruction as "teaching and learning mediated by a computer". Online education is primarily Internet based education. Generally the world wide web (www) is the main communication tool through other un-integrated media like e-mail. Online learning may involve two distinct forms, namely, resource based learning that is electronically delivered, and "virtual classroom" learning using computer based synchronous and asynchronous conferencing (Inglis,1999, Jegede, 2001). Online learning makes use of computer mediated communication including e-mail, computer conferencing, online databases and file transfers.

Quality of good Online Moderator

Online knowledge moderators stimulate participation in an online knowledge community. They are aware of different knowledge transfer patterns and differing needs of people. Moderator's goal is to help a community to become self-sufficient. Online knowledge moderators have to be very good "listeners". They need to read all online postings carefully and seek clarification when necessary. Good moderators keep in contact with other moderators. They help members in expanding their knowledge.

Virtual University

A Virtual university is one which delivers all its services across electronic networks. The platform is the infrastructure including hardware and software to deliver the teaching material, to administer the system and to provide communication services. Most current systems only provide a small part of these services via electronic networks. Origin of Virtual Education in India, Tamil Virtual University (TVU) is the first in Tamil Nadu, followed by IGNOU and other universities like Punjab Technical University and number of private corporate and other Associations like AIMA, etc.

The components of a Virtual University system are as follows

- A layer presents general information (usually not protected)
- A layer presents the teaching material (usually protected)

- A layer to facilitate communication among the different sectors of the virtual university by e.g. e-mail, news groups or chat and videoconferencing (partially protected)
- Technical infrastructure

Flexibility and adaptiveness will be important as well as a client centered approach of teaching and counseling in Virtual University system.

The virtual university needs a common platform to integrate all its services. Actually platform has the following subsystems.

- Information system
- Communication system
- Teaching system
- Library services
- Administration system

These different tasks are also represented by the respective server structure. That means servers to administer the Web pages, data bank-server for course administration and enrollment and servers for communication. Students want to study materials that are available online. Students visiting the university's home page may be already familiar with the general Web-Information about the study system and therefore can access immediately their virtual study site. By entering this site they either have a first look at the available courses or they may identify themselves with a personal password to see their individual courses and download or study them online.

Communication Component

Apart from e-mail access to faculty or regional tutors an ample system of news group has been established on the university news server. News groups do exists for each course, for informal discussion groups, for online seminars and for tutorial support.

Chat and Video Conferencing

Other important communication tools are chat and videoconferences. Chat is mainly used for small group tutoring and counseling. Multipoint videoconferences were used for tutorials with large audiences in specially prepared lecture halls. Another application is to take oral examination with remote study centres through videoconferencing. This type of examinations are economic and attractive to students.

Virtual Seminars

Seminars usually are held at a fixed date and time and at a fixed location. So far this type of seminar is considered as an indispensable element of academic teaching. Therefore it forms part of university education even in distance teaching environments. Today, virtual seminars gain increasing importance as a complement and in part as a substitution of traditional face-to-face seminars. Papers or other results elaborated by students are presented through networks. The location of the seminar is the internet. Participants communicate through personal computers with Internet access from home, work place or regional study center.

Learning Materials: The success of an online programme is greatly dependent upon the course content, curriculum design and learning material.

Computer Based Evaluation

Due to the advancement of science and technology some innovative evaluation methods are developed during the last decade. With the help of computer in which the computer will generate the required number of questions for each student and the students will answer for the questions through key board was developed. But this method can be used only in the closed circuit system, in which the master computer and the monitors are interconnected.

Online Evaluation

Online evaluation is a modern trend, used to evaluate the performance of the learners like learning attainment, progress in the projects, research works, acquiring skills.

E-mail based evaluation: Using this techniques questions may be send to the learners and the learners may send their answer to the examiner through e-mail.

Chat based evaluation: In this techniques the questions and answers are exchanged instantaneously between the examiner and the learner.

Video Conference based evaluation: In this techniques the images of both the examiner and examinee will appear on the monitor and both will exchange the questions, answers and explanations etc., in alive telecast manner.

Web based evaluation: Using this techniques the learners individually access the test items available in the website and send their answers to the same website.

Challenges

Online/virtual education is more popular among the student community. At present the on-line evaluation is implemented effectively in higher education level. As an emerging trend, we have to face some challenges during the implementation of the on-line evaluation techniques like,

- Need of infrastructure facilities like, well equipped separate Internet laboratory
- Need of a separate website.

- Need of trained teachers in various applications of the Internet.
- Need to provide adequate training to students in the basic skills related to operation of computer and Internet.
- Need to develop the required software for the specific online evaluation techniques.
- Need to evalue the required paradigm for each techniques.
- Negative attitude against the new approaches.
- Lack of adequate number of experts for planning and implementation.

Future Perspectives

Curriculum reform to upgrade standards at the international level should be done at periodical interval. It is also required to maintain competitiveness in an international educational market also. It will have to move fast ahead to cope with the upcoming supply of web-courses from traditional universities. A few universities in the developing countries have started offering online courses while many others are contemplating as a major activity in the near future. While doing so it will be necessary for them to plan carefully taking into consideration all factors.

As in the case of most other activities there is a growing concern about the quality of online programme being offered the world over. While it is presumed that proper infrastructure in the form of media-centre, library, technology-support, faculty etc., will be available, the university will have to identify the most important elements of an online course and accordingly control the design, development and production of learning materials. Student support services will have to be carefully monitored, and due attention will have to be directed to staff training and development.

There was a strong demand made in various quarters for the establishment of an open university which could coordinate the work of all the directorates in the country. It was also felt that an apex institution of this kind fully devoted to the development of distance education would be very useful. Therefore, IGNOU came into existence and a detailed description and discussion regarding to the establishment of Indira Gandhi National Open University are given below:

Indira Gandhi National Open University (IGNOU)

The National Policy on Education (1986) of the Government of India stressed the importance of non-formal system of education to expand the educational facilities in the country. It is also proposed to strengthen distance education institutions and improve their quality. The IGNOU has been charged with the responsibility of promoting open university and distance education systems in the country. The idea of establishing an open university to offer quality education to the "much larger body of population which remains outside the university system" was proposed as early as 1970 in a seminar. Co-sponsored by the ministry of Information and Broadcasting and the UGC, following the recommendation of the seminar, the government of India appointed an eight member working group with G. Parthasarthy, the then Vice-Chancellor of Jawarhalal Nehru University, as Chairman. After a decade IGNOU was established on 20th September, 1985, under an Act of Parliament. The Indira Gandhi National Open University has been established with laudable objectives and its scope is very wide. This is evident from the following provisions of the Act. The objectives of the university shall be to advance and disseminate learning, and learning by a diversity of means, including the use of any communication technology, to provide opportunities for higher education to a large segment of the population and to promote the educational well being of the community generally to encourage the Open University and Distance education system in the educational pattern of the country and to coordinate and determine the standards in such systems..." (Indira Gandhi National Open University Act, 1985). IGNOU is a National University which develops and produces courses for delivery using open learning methods. It offers programmes that lead to degrees, diplomas, certificates. IGNOU invariably serves for the fulfillment of the objectives of life-long education, universal literacy, adult and continuing education and the future thrust of the government in the direction of distance and open learning to provide opportunities to the youth, housewives, agricultural and industrial workers and professional to continue the education of their choice at the pace suited to them, the initiation of open university system in order to augment opportunities for higher education and as instrument of democratizing education. IGNOU is an apex body for open universities and distance education institutions in the country charged with the responsibilities of the promotion and coordination of the distance education system. IGNOU Act provided for establishment of Distance Education Council (DEC) and Staff Training and Research Institute for Distance Education (STRIDE).

The IGNOU has been the recipient of support from a number of international agencies such as:

1. The Overseas Development Administration (ODA), U.K.
2. Japan International Cooperation Agency (J1CA), Japan.
3. The Commonwealth of Learning (COL), Canada.

IGNOU comes directly under the purview of the Ministry of Human Resource development for financial assistance and other supports.

Features of the IGNOU

The principles of Open University Learning through distance education form the philosophical and pragmatic base of the University. The significant features of IGNOU are:

- National Character of jurisdiction.
- Flexible academic qualification for admission to Bachelors Degree.
- Individualized study, Flexibility of place, pace and time of study.
- Use of modern educational and communication technology including audio-video components, computers and broadcast media.
- Student Support Services.
- A comprehensive evaluation scheme.
- Extensive electronic inputs and intensive counseling sessions.

Organizational structure of IGNOU

The board of management is similar to the executive council in the central universities. The president of India is the visitor of the university. The officers of the university are the Vice-chancellor, the Pro Vice-chancellors, the directors, the registrars and the finance officer. The organizational structure is given in the chart. 1.2.

Administration of Learning Packages of IGNOU

IGNOU's main campus is planned within the easy proximity for the broadcasting facilities of All Indio Radio and Doordarshan. It has a well-equipped library with a modern reprographic service units, and a translation center attached to the library. Among the different components of the

CHART NO. 1.2

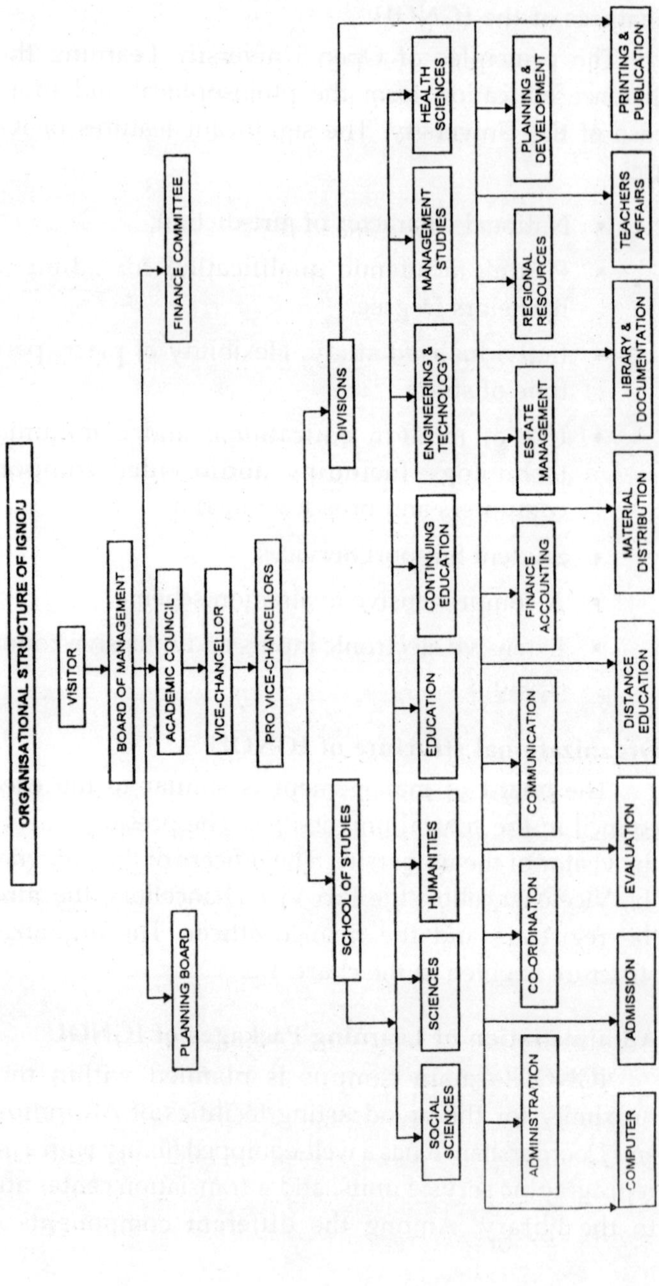

ORGANISATIONAL STRUCTURE OF IGNOU
VISITOR
BOARD OF MANAGEMENT
FINANCE COMMITTEE
PLANNING BOARD
ACADEMIC COUNCIL
VICE-CHANCELLOR
PRO VICE-CHANCELLORS
SCHOOL OF STUDIES
SOCIAL SCIENCES
SCIENCES
HUMANITIES
EDUCATION
CONTINUING EDUCATION
ENGINEERING & TECHNOLOGY
MANAGEMENT STUDIES
HEALTH SCIENCES
DIVISIONS
COMPUTER
ADMINISTRATION
ADMISSION
CO-ORDINATION
EVALUATION
COMMUNICATION
DISTANCE EDUCATION
FINANCE ACCOUNTING
MATERIAL DISTRIBUTION
ESTATE MANAGEMENT
LIBRARY & DOCUMENTATION
REGIONAL RESOURCES
TEACHERS AFFAIRS
PLANNING & DEVELOPMENT
PRINTING & PUBLICATION

administrative system (a) the dispatch-unit (b) printing and publication unit, and (c) the postal unit play a very important role.

Year-wise Enrolment of Learners in IGNOU

The learner's enrolment is rapidly increasing in IGNOU because of its openness and flexibility. The table 1.5 shows the year-wise enrolment of learners in IGNOU.

TABLE 1.5

Year-wise Enrolment

Year	*1996*	*1997*	*1998*	*1999*	*2000*	*2001*	*2002*	*2003*
Enrolment	130200	162500	163400	172500	196650	291360	301724	316547
Growth diff. in Nos.	38800	32300	900	9100	24150	94750	10364	14823
Growth diff. in %	42.45%	24.81%	0.55%	5.57%	14.00%	48.18%	3.56%	4.91%

Academic Programmes

IGNOU offers both short-term and long-term programmes in the areas of general education, provides continuing education, extension education facilities for research also. These programmes leads to certificate, diploma, graduate, postgraduate and research degrees. Flexibility is the corner stone of the IGNOU. There are two streams of learners non-formal (who do not have any qualification) and formal (those who have the requisite qualification). Another important feature of the courses is that all courses are prepared in the form of credits. Bachelor's preparatory programme (BPP) aims at preparing those who do not have formal qualification for admission to Bachelor's degree. The learners enrolled in this programme have to qualify in an entrance test. In preparing and launching the Bachelor's Degree Programme (BDF), a number of schools are involved. In 2002-03, 1235 Audio and 1520 Video Programmes are produced by IGNOU. Various Programmes offered by IGNOU as shown in the chart. 1.3.

CHART NO. 1.3

Programmes offered in IGNOU

I. Doctor of Philosophy

1. Education (Ph.D.Ed.)
2. Economics (Ph.D.)
3. History/Tourism Studies (Ph.D.)
4. Library & Information Science (Ph.D)
5. Public Administration (Ph.D.)
6. Sociology (Ph.D.)
7. Political Science (Ph.D.)
8. Integrated Doctoral Program in Physics & Mathematics (Ph.D)

II. Bachelor's Degree & Master's Degree Programs

1. Master in English (MEG)
2. Master in Hindi (MIID)
3. Bachelor of Arts (BA)
4. Bachelor of Commerce (B.Com)
5. Bachelor of Science (B.Sc.)
6. Bachelor's Preparatory Program Leading to BA, B.Com. for non 10+2(BPP)
7. Bachelor in Nautical Science Leading to B.Sc. Nautical Science

III. Computer and Library & Information Sciences

1. Master in Computer Applications (MCA)
2. Master in Library and Information Science (MLIS)
3. Bachelor in Computer Applications (BCA)
4. Bachelor in Information Technology (BIT)
5. Advanced Diploma in Information Technology (ADIT)
6. P.G. Diploma in Library Automation & Networking
7. Certificate in Computing (CIC).
8. Computer Literacy Program (CLP)

IV. Journalism, Communication and Creative Writing

1. P.G. Diploma in Translation (PGDT)
2. P.G. Certificate in Radio Writing (PGCR)
3. P.G. Diploma in Journalism and Mass Communication (PGJMC)
4. P.G. Diploma in Audio Program Production (PGDAPP)
5. Radio Prasaran Mein Snatakottar Diploma (PGDRP)

5\. Diploma in Creative Writing in English (DCE)

6\. Diploma in Creative Writing in Hindi (DCH)

V. Health, Nutrition & Child Care

1. Bachelor of Science in Nursing (B.Sc. N)
2. Bachelor of Science in Hospitality & Hotel Admn. (BHA)
3. P.G. Diploma in Maternal and Child Health (PGDMCH)
4. P.G. Diploma in Hospital and Health Management (PGDIIHM)
5. P.G. Diploma in Geriatric Medicine (PGDGM)
6. Diploma in Early Childhood Care and Education (DECE)
7. Diploma in Nutrition & Health Education (DNIIE)
8. Diploma in HIV and Family Education (DAFE)
9. Certificate in HIV and Family Education (CAFE)
10. Certificate in Nutrition and Child Care (CNCC)
11. Certificate in Food & Nutrition (CFN)
12. P.G. Certificate in Rural Surgery (PGCRS)

VI. Engineering & Rural Development

1. Bachelor in Technology in Civil (Construction Management) (BTCM)
2. Bachelor in Technology in Civil (Water Resource Engineering) (BTWRE)
3. Advanced Diploma in Construction Management (ADCM)
4. Advanced Diploma in Water Resources Engineering (ADWRE)
5. P. G. Diploma in Rural Development (PGDRD)
6. Certificate in Rural Development (CRD)

VII. Education & Distance Education

1. Master of Arts in Distance Education (MADE)
2. Bachelor of Education (B. Ed)
3. P. G. Diploma in Higher Education (PGDHE)
4. P.G. Diploma in Distance Education.(PGDDE)
5. Diploma in Primary Education (DPE)
6. Certificate in Guidance (CIG)
7. Certificate in Teaching of Primary School Mathematics (CTPM)
8. Certificate in the Teaching of English (CTE)
9. Certificate in Primary Education (CPE)

VIII. Management & Tourism Studies

1. Master of Business Administration in HRD/ Finance/ Operations/Marketing (MBA)
2. Master of Business Administration (Banking & Finance) (MBF)
3. Commonwealth (executive Master of Business Administration (CEMBA)
4. Commonwealth Executive Master of Public Administration (CEMPA)
5. Master in Tourism Management (MTM)
6. Bachelor in Tourism Studies (BTS)
7. P.G. Diploma in Management (PGD1M)
8. P.G. Diploma in Human Resource Management (PGDHRM)
9. I'.G. Diploma in Financial Management (PGDFM)
10. P.G. Diploma in Operations Management (PGDOM)
11. P.G. Diploma in Marketing Management (PGDMM)
12. P.G. Diploma in International Business Operations (PGDIBO)
13. Diploma in Management (DIM)
14. Diploma in Tourism Studies (DTS)
15. Certificate in Tourism Studies (CTS)

IX. Women and Youth Development

1. Diploma in Youth in Development Work (DCYP)
2. Certificate in Empowering Women through Self Help Groups (CWDL)
3. Certificate in Women's Empowerment and Development (CWED)
4. Certificate in Youth in Development Work (CCYP)

X. Area Specific Awareness & Manpower Development Programs

1. P.G. Certificate in Participatory Management of Displacement Resettlement and Rehabilitation (PGCMRR)
2. Certificate in Disaster Management (CDM)
3. Certificate in Environmental Studies (CES)
4. Certificate in Participatory Forest Management (CPFM)
5. Certificate in Labour Development (CLD)
6. Certificate in Human Rights (CIIR)
7. Certificate in Consumer Protection (CCP)
8. Certificate in Laboratory Techniques (CPLT)
9. Certificate in Participatory Project Planning (SAVINI)
10. Awareness Course on Intellectual Property Rights

Admission Procedures

The open education system does not fix any basic academic qualifications as eligibility criterion for the purpose of admission to a university level academic courses for a degree or diploma or certificate. This admission procedure can help millions of those who cannot obtain the degree or diploma or certificate because of one or other reason other, but now mature enough and highly motivated to undergo higher education courses.

Instructional Material

The university makes use of modern communication technology as well as developments in educational technology to impart quality education to its distance learners. The university is a multi-media university using printed texts, radio and T.V. broadcasting, audio-visual aids, home experiment kits and face-to-face teaching. The course materials are prepared by the team of experts who are mostly drawn from the conventional universities. They are advised in the preparation of the courses by the experts in educational technology from the division of distance education. The package of audio and video materials are also decided by them. The various instructional strategies used by IGNOU are indicated in chart 1.4.

Staffing Pattern at IGNOU

The academic and non-academic staff of IGNOU is different from that of the conventional universities. It has full time staff, part-time staff and consultants. It has full-time staff at the head office and regional centers. The study centers are manned by part-time staff only. Services of distinguished scholars are availed either on full-time basis or on part-time basis for consultations and producing quality educational programmes.

CHART 1.4

INSTRUCTIONAL SYSTEMS AT IGNOU

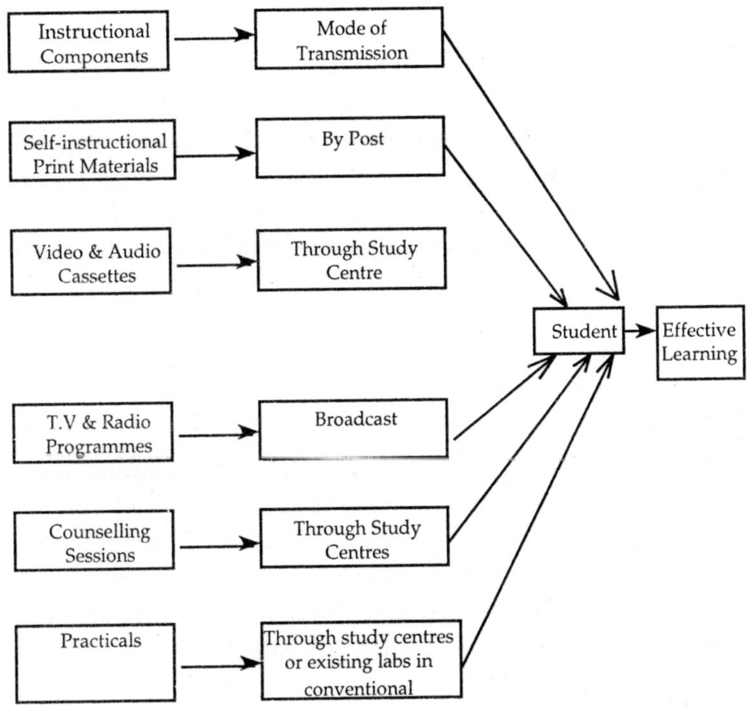

Source: Development in Distance Education in Asia, UNESCO/ICDE 1989

Regional Centres

Regional centres play a very pivotal role in the organizational structure of the university. The regional centers are the intermediaries between the central institution and local study centers. IGNOU has 48 regional centres (including PG regional centres). Each regional center functions with a Regional Director and Assistant Regional Directors. The Regional centers have number of functions like Academic promotional role, Learners admissions, Appointment of part time counsellors, Summer/Winter schools, Staff development programmes, Management and Conduct of Examinations, Coordination and supervision of study centres, etc.

Supporting Service Systems

Study Centre

The study centres constitute the most important link between the learners and counselors and between a university and the academic staff responsible for providing counselling, and evaluation of internal assignment. IGNOU has 1081 study centres spread all over India.

Counselling

It is at the study center, the learners have the best opportunities for obtaining counselling of all kinds, as there is access to advice from subject specialists, help for improving study skills, to obtain information about choice of courses and assistance for non-academic problems. The major functions of an academic counsellors are (i) Academic Counselling (ii) Use of multi-media (iii) Evaluation of assignments. IGNOU has 25500 Academic Counsellors spread all over India.

Library

The library is a very powerful instrument for academic growth and development of distance education. IGNOU has a well equipped central library and documentation facilities with a collection of 50,000 books and 400 journals. This university provides strong support to its learners, by providing library facilities at the regional as well as study centres. Books are also kept for reference at the study center library.

Printed Study Materials

Indira Gandhi National Open University's approach to production of study material is based on team concept, with subject experts, language specialists, professional from printing unit etc. Therefore, IGNOU has been able to produce high quality study materials in an attractive error-free manner.

Non-Print Materials

Indira Gandhi National Open University is using media to supplement the role of counsellors. Radio as a medium of instruction is quite important because the voice of the radio can be heard even in those parts where there is no library, educational institute or newspapers and therefore IGNOU has started broadcasting in English and Hindi from Hyderabad, Bombay and Shillong. Similarly IGNOU has started telecasting its programmes on the television from May 20, 1991. In view of the success and credibility of the system the ministries of HRD and Information and Broadcasting, Government of India have provided extensive support to the system by encouraging and facilitating phenomenal growth of T.V. and Radio broadcast system in the form of a bouquets of Gyan Darshan TV channels and Gyan vani FM Radio stations with IGNOU as the National Nodal center.

Audio and Video cassettes are very important means of instructions in distance education. IGNOU has been explaining these channels of communications. The print material is supported by these video and audio cassettes and explanations are given by the subject expert wherever required. Audio and Video cassettes are produced by the communication division and there has been a steady growth in audio programmes every year. All the study centres receive multi-media packages. One of the IGNOU video programmes entitled the Victorian era won the first prize at the national level competition organized by the University Grants Commission.

Evaluation

The evaluation division is involved in operations of massive proportions. The terminal examinations are held in December and June. IGNOU learners go through a process of continuous assessment involving tutor-marked assignment and computer-marked assignments.

Scope and Objectives of the Study

It is evident that million of learners who opt for the mode of distance education facilities are a different clientele group and expect quality delivery system. Therefore their perception, attitudes and outlook need to be taken care of while serving these groups. The Open University through its distance mode of education has immense promise and potential because of its great flexibility and high productivity.

The open learning systems and their contribution to non-formal and formal education systems across the globe has been considered effective and efficacious. As regards the Indian situation, there is need to describe the operational strategies or programmes and supporting systems for the purpose of designing it properly and also methodologically to fulfill the social, academic and economic objectives of open learning systems keeping the above rationale. Hence the study in this area help to see how far the open learning principles have been successfully achieved in terms of its objectives, goal and supporting systems such as self-instructional materials, multi-media approach, infrastructure and evaluation techniques.

General Objectives

1. To study the socio-economic characteristics of the distance learners, who are involved in this study.
2. To study the attitude of distance learners with regard to several variables of the open university

Specific Objectives

1. To study the attitude of distance learners with regard to admission procedures of IGNOU.

2. To study the attitude of distance learners in study centres towards selected the six aspects* of IGNOU programmes.
3. To study the attitude of distance learners pursuing different types of programmes towards the six aspects* of IGNOU programmes.
4. To study the attitude of distance learners with regard to printed self-instructional materials provided by IGNOU.
5. To study the attitude of distance learners with regard to non-print study materials with particular reference to Television programmes provided by IGNOU.
6. To study the attitude of distance learners with regard to Study Centres and Library facilities provided by IGNOU.
7. To study the attitude of distance learners with regard to Counsellor and Counselling activities conducted by IGNOU.
8. To study the attitude of distance learners with regard to Evaluation: (Assignment and Examinations) conducted by IGNOU

Operational Definitions

Operational definitions have been provided for certain technical terms used in this book.

Distance Education: According to Holmberg (1977) the term Distance education covers the various forms of study at all levels which are not under the continuous immediate supervision of tutors present with their learners in lecture

---

*Six aspects of IGNOU programme

(1) Admission Procedures (2) Printed Self-Instructional Material (3) Non-Print Material - IGNOU Television Programmes (4) Study Centre and Library Facilities (5) Counsellor and Counselling and (6) Evaluation: Assignment and Examinations.

room or on the same premises, but which nevertheless benefit from the planning guidance and tuition of the tutorial organization,

Open Learning System: UNESCO (1975) describes Open Learning System as follows: "such as systems (that) are designed to offer opportunities for learning at distance for innovations in the curriculum. Open University System aims to redress social or educational inquires and to offer opportunities not provided by conventional colleges or universities."

Attitude: Allport (1935) defines attitude as a mental and neural state of readiness, exerting a directive influence upon the individual's response to all subjects and situations with which it is related.

According to Sills (1968) "An attitude is a relatively enduring organization of beliefs around an object or situation predisposing one to respond in some preferential manner."

Counselling: Maslow defines counselling "A segmatic exploration of self and environment by a client with the aid of a counsellor to clarify self-understanding and environmental alternatives so that behaviour modifications or decisions".

Programmes: The term programme (s) has been used to mean the courses offered by IGNOU.

Limitation of the Study

1. Those who were enrolled during the year 1991.
2. The study is limited to four IGNOU study centres in Tamil Nadu.

This introductory chapter presents an overview of formal and non-formal education system with particular reference to distance education and open learning systems in India and other countries.

2

Studies on Open University Systems

Research studies related to concept and theory, structure and organization, media of communications, supporting systems and evaluation procedures, research staff training and development are presented.

Concept and Theory of Distance/Open University Education in Abroad

Daniel (1991) defines the term "open university" as a form of instruction in which class room sessions are not the primary means of communications, to call an educational offering "open learning" is confusing unless the context indicates the dimension of openness that is to be understood properly.

Garrison *et al.*, (1987) assert that learners have the freedom to make choices. They are also of the opinion that distance learners have the ability and skills to take responsibility for learning and access to resources necessary for learning.

Hawkins (1976) says that the Open University has become a success story. It has also faced disaster, even abolition. It has been seen as a political plaything, an educational gimmicks, a technological monster and a costly proposition.

Henriet, *et al.*, (1985) argue that one of the main tasks of distance/open education is to foster not only the ability to work independently but also to maintain learners autonomy, the exercise of personal choice, etc.

Kaye (1981) outlined the features of autonomous distance teaching institutions, of which the primary component in open universities are

- Teaching, assessment and accreditation functions are integrated.
- The institution is totally committed to external students and there is a strong motivation to develop and enhance distance methods free from the constraints and traditions of face-to-face teaching.
- The institution is in principle far free to devise new educational programmes for new target groups and to explore to the maximum potential of distance education methods in so doing.
- The institution is also free to choose teaching methods and media curricula course structure, assessment procedures and accreditation polices etc.

According to Omloewa (1984) the National Open University (NOU) is one of the latest member institutions of the International Council for Distance Education (ICDE). The scope of the National Open University work is however unparalleled in Africa in terms of target audience and spread of programmes. Before the National Open University was established, conventional universities had played a major role in higher education.

The National Open University is the first of its type, wholly devoted to the execution of the distance education system and committed to providing access to higher education for men and women in Nigeria who are estimated to be 53 million. It is also actively considering the need to work closer with Nigeria National Council for Adult Education, which has been consistently supportive of the Open University Systems in Africa.

Paul (1989) opines that more institutions are practicing open learning techniques, delivering in non-traditional ways to off-campus students, and trying to use new technologies to improve the existing practices. "Open" education institutions are very much in vogue in the United Kingdom at present, with much discussion about the differences among "Open Learning", "Distance Education", and "Distance Study" technologies.

Reddy (1986) asserts that distance learning will be a boon to dropouts of formal education, married young women whose attitudes and emerging economic trends will compel them to study for better opportunities and those in remote areas where higher education facilities do not exist at all. The teaching methodology consists of a four-fold segmentation involving 65 per cent of a systematic reading, 10 per cent of audio-visual (Radio and T.V.) exposure, 15 per cent of contact study and the rest by practical. With this background we find four important ingredients intimately interwoven in the basic fabric of distance education.

- The courses prepared must be of a very high order, better than the existing university courses.
- Use of effective delivery system.
- Availability of continuous feedback from students; and
- Research facilities to cater to the needs of post-graduate students.

An effective delivery system is one of the most needed vital segments of distance education and hence we have to utilize the existing mass media like the radio and television. Programmatic planning, scientific thinking, honesty, good quality of material and an effective delivery system, with continuous feedback are the other ingredients that should also be ensured for the success of an Open University. Institutional interests should weigh supreme, then only the National Open University will achieve the set goals and become a pre-eminent institution.

Rumble *et al.*, (1982) have identified the following characteristics of distance teaching universities.

- The use of a wide range of media and other resources to teach, necessitating a variety of production and distribution systems appropriate to the media in use.
- Associated with the use of various media, a marked role differentiation of staff.
- In a number of systems, a marked division of labour between those responsible for materials design and production on the one hand, and those responsible for tuition and assessment on the other.
- The centralized design and production of materials combined with localized learning.
- The provision of two-way communication between students and tutors who generally operate at a distance from the students but with the possibility of occasional meetings between students and tutors (face to face tuition), thus imposing on the institutions a need to organize and control those channels to ensure both effective and efficient operation.
- The introduction into an academic community of a number of quasi-industrial processes, which require appropriate management techniques, and a hierarchical government structure of management and control, which does not ways, relate easily to traditional forms of university governance.
- Extensive and well defined administrative areas.

Taylor (1983) feels that the open universities have come to stay and have demonstrated their capability to cater to the needs of the people, who for some reason or other cannot pursue studies in conventional streams. It has been acknowledged world over that education should not be a 'strait-jacket' cramping the style of the students. Further, he says that technology is merely a means, the end being good education, for which a good teacher is needed and a good teacher is hard to come by these days. Although it is highly costly in the initial stages, "distance education" is economical in the long run. He feels that by and large, correspondence courses do not offer proper teaching materials. Hence visual medium like television can make a better impact on distance learners than other known media.

In India

In a brief overview, Adiseshiah (1992) provides glimpses of "the growth and development of distance education in India". He distinguishes three kinds of major distance education programme such as correspondence education, providing regular formal credential oriented programmes through correspondence; Radio education (a second of distance education) providing agricultural extension programme to farmers and finally, television education providing advance science courses for student at the graduate and post graduate levels, as is being done in India and elsewhere.

Further, Adiseshiah opines that there are strong points in these programmes. They are:

- Provide access to those who cannot afford full-time programme.
- Cover vast distance.
- Ensure high quality learning.
- Economical and optimal use of resources.

- Provide opportunity to learners to learn at their own pace.

His analysis also includes the following weaknesses of distance education system.

- Absence of one-to-one relationship.
- Non-inclusion of certain subjects.
- Commercialization of the system.

Dutt (1989) states in his study "Distance Education AD 2000" that the figure for higher education will raise to 7.83 per cent, 5.95 per cent for the enrollment in universities and colleges, and 1.85 per cent for enrollment in distance education. It may be noted that India is far behind the developed countries in the race for providing higher education. With the rapid growth of distance education in the next decade, the supply constraint will become relatively less operative and the urge for higher education will be satisfied by this relatively cheap technology of higher education.

Further, Dutt (1993) has given the following suggestions:

- Distance education programme should be developed as an integral part of the university's teaching mission, not in a separate division devoted to the teaching of off-campus students.
- Teachers in the university's teaching departments should be the primary resource persons for writing and revising the academic content of course materials for distance education programmes. In doing this, they should work with members of distance learning center which would be the university's repository of current knowledge of the theory and practice of distance education; They should have relevant expertise for the planning and production of distance education study programmes; and they should also

have administrative responsibility for the effective conduct of the university's distance education activities.

- Distance education activities should be conducted in relation to plans and priorities and under policies and working arrangements that have the full authority of the university and they should be properly funded, monitored, and regularly evaluated.
- As and when required, all university teachers should be expected to participate in distance as well as campus programmes and therefore, contracts of appointment should be written accordingly.
- The contributions that a university's teachers make to its distance education programmes should be planned and administered as a regular part of their teaching duties. There should be university rules for moderating teaching loads so that teachers are not penalized by the nature of their teaching, whether it is face-to face, distance or some mixture of both.
- There should be continuing programme of staff development relating to distance education.
- The university should ensure that its criteria for the purposes of staff assessment and promotion allow its teachers to induce their contributions to distance education among their claims to consideration.
- The university's polices for improving the effectiveness of its teaching, including distance teaching, should be set in the context of research, development and evaluation.

Devi *et al.*, (1994) lay emphasis on implementing the programmes, as they are cost effective in distance education. She is also of the opinion that distance education may be best suited to vocationalise education aiming at the literate and neo-literate adult learner with relevant occupational experience.

According to Kulandaiswamy (1994) the Open University System has gained relevance in the context of modern day changes.

- Providing education to all ensuring equality and providing continuing or life-long education.
- The conventional university is not designed to meet these challenges which also call for education that is cost effective, flexible and ensure high productivity.

Kulandaiswamy further asserts that the distance education transforms teaching from a stage of a craft to that of technology.

Rao (1994) asserts that distance education is not a cheap alternate to formal education. It is an education, which is even more sophisticated, more difficult to achieve formal education. Large number of students who are spread all over the state, or the country as the case may be, find it sometimes baffling how they can cope with this learning that is being imparted from a distance through several media, through gadgets, and whether it is possible for them to understand the subjects as thoroughly as in regular education.

Pandit (1994) in her paper "A vision for higher education through distance education in India" makes an attempt to explore the strategies to make distance education more accessible and responsive to the variety of demands on higher education front in India. She focuses on some important aspects like:

(a) Status of higher education system in India, in terms of quality and access.

(b) Emerging learning needs and expectations of 21st century.

(c) Advantages of distance education.

(d) Drawbacks of distance education in India.

Based on the drawbacks of the distance education system and higher education system as a whole, Pandit has suggested some strategies to make distance education system in India more effective and responsive to the emerging needs of the society. Distance education has got many advantages like

- Improving the quality of labour force,
- Increasing work efficiency and productivity,
- Providing better employment opportunity,
- Minimizing opportunity cost and contributing to equity and equal opportunity.

Pathusa (1992) says that the Distance Education Council (DEC) structure and organization being still in its early stages, it has come to stay as the apex body for the distance education institutions in India. Although brought into existence by the IGNOU, the DEC is expected to have natural character on par with the UGC. The functions to be performed by DEC are the promotion, Co-ordination, determination of standards of open university/distance education systems.

Raj (1994) states that as the open university systems are controlled and financed by their respective universities, they have no freedom to frame their syllabus or make innovation in their system of examination. The UGC deals with distance education separately from other departments of teaching and research in the universities and it has prescribed special rules for the financial grants to the distance education institutions on the recommendations of its inspection committee.

Swaminathan (1994) describes the efficiency of various approaches of distance education stressing that

- The existing duel mode universities could be encouraged to strengthen their distance education programmes,

- The other conventional universities may also be encouraged to offer distance education programmes,
- Each State should establish an open university and the IGNOU should provide technical and consultancy support to the state government for this purpose. It should also provide course material prepared by it to other open university,
- The UGC should review the existing rules for providing central assistance to open universities,
- The Distance Education Council should prepare guidelines for providing financial support to state open universities for their development.

The Vice-Chancellors Round Table (1994) on "Quality assurance in distance education" prepared an action plan to provide effective distance education in this country. The action to be initiated have been grouped under the following three categories:

- Action to be taken by the university concerned
- Action to be taken by the correspondence/distance education unit
- The responsibility of the apex bodies, University Grants Commission (UGC) and the Distance Education Council (DEC).
- The universities concerned will appoint an Advisory Committee for the distance education units as recommended by the UGC.
- The universities concerned will develop detailed job descriptions specifying the duties and responsibility of the heads of the distance education units and send it to the UGC.
- The universities concerned will develop plans to ensure the mobility of students from the distance stream to the conventional stream and vice-versa.

- The universities will prepare plans for conducting training programmes, transforming materials, developing training materials out of the surplus, if any, accruing out of the activities of the distance education unit.
- The universities will actively encourage the staff of the distance education units to take training in distance education activities.
- The universities will explore the feasibility of converting some portion of the degree requirements to the distance mode and make it possible for students to combine the distance and the face-to-face components.
- The universities will make plans to computerize certain essential operations of the distance education units.

Action to be taken by the Correspondence/Distance Education Unit

- Each of the participating Correspondence Course Institutes (CCIs) will transform about 15 per cent of their course materials into self-instructional formats.
- Each distance education unit will establish a mechanism for the systematic dissemination of information about its programmes. Such a mechanism will have a name like Information Cell or Publicity Cell as appropriate.
- Each of the participating CCIs will identify and include in their instructional packages at least 25 videos made by the UGC countrywide classroom project.
- Each of the participating CCIs will develop detailed curricula for at least two innovative and or employment/skill oriented programmes/courses.
- To produce a proposal about the action each one can

take to disseminate upgradation to those who did not participate in the recent seminar/round table.

Responsibility of the Apex Bodies

- To develop norms regarding the physical facilities.
- To make resources available for training.
- To develop innovations regarding course structure.
- To develop certain courses centrally, e.g., a course on women's issues may be developed by SNDT and disseminated to other universities.
- To initiate the sharing of the resources of audio-visual production facilities in the Education Media Research Centres and Audio Visual Research Centres.
- To develop a policy regarding accreditation procedures.
- Development of a strategy to disseminate the quality assurance culture to the rest of the conventional universities (having correspondence course institutes) by identifying regional leader.

STRUCTURE AND ORGANISATION

In abroad—Asian Countries

The commitment to distance education is especially strong in Asia. Open Universities, or Autonomous institution making extensive use of communications technologies, have been established in at least nine countries - China, Hong Kong, India, Indonesia, Israel, Pakistan, Korea, Sri Lanka and Thailand and dual mode universities provide distance education programmes in a number of countries including Bangladesh, China, India and Malaysia. Three of the four countries, with which this study is concerned, have had experience of distance education and/or media based teaching since 1960 or earlier.

China

China's distance learning system has its own characteristics. The national, multimedia distance learning institution of China is called the Central Radio and Television University (CRTVU). During 1960's television universities were set up in Beijing, Shanghai, Shenyang and some other cities in order to provide a convenient means for adult students to improve their education. Television University in Beijing in 1979 which is at present one of the largest distance education institutes in the world with well over a million students on its rolls. Television Programmes are transmitted by the Central China Television (CCTV), nationally through the micro-wave network. Television class also organize courses taught by part time tutors who some times also use audio or video tapes produced by the CRTVU. For social science courses radio is the chief medium.

Indonesia

In Indonesia a national programme was introduced in 1984 for primary school children. The first programme was based on self-instructional materials, including printed texts, audio cassettes, slides and radio broadcasts. At second level, conventional junior high school provides instruction as part of the open junior high school programme (Selim, 1986). Students are supervised by a tutor, and follow the same curriculum as the regular high school. As in somewhat similar programmes in a number of African countries, the tutor does not teach but facilitate learning by organizing, supporting and motivating students. Students attend at the regular high school one day each week for face-to face instruction with teacher. The University of Terbuka was established in 1984.

Korea

Distance learning projects exist in Korea both in formal and non-formal distance education. Much of the non-formal distance education in Korea comes through the broadcast media and in work-related self-improvement seminars and workshops. In 1974, eleven AIR and correspondence high schools were attached to existing conventional high schools throughout Korea. The Korea AIR and Correspondence University (KACU) began much like the AIR and correspondence high schools, attached to a parent organization, Seoul National University. The university began by offering two years junior college course in nine departments. In 1984, the number had grown to thirteen diverse programmes. The media employed in teaching the courses are:

a. *Written material:* Correspondence texts, supplementary materials and the university newspaper,
b. *Audio-visual materials:* Radio and television broadcasts, audio and video cassettes,
c. *Schooling:* Compulsory sessions held at cooperating institutions for testing lectures and practical or experimental work.
d. *Special lectures:* Professors and special guest lecturers. The Korea AIR and correspondence university has been in a constant state of adjustment in order to meet the needs of the university and its student body. To fulfill the need of students for a place to study and to meet the regional centers were given priority. And to satisfy the need for personal contact between professors and students, the schooling was created.

Pakistan

The Allama Iqbal Open University (AIOU) is a unique distance teaching institution. Besides being the oldest in South Asia, the AIOU is broadly modeled on the British Open University. It has made a great impact on the educational scene of Pakistan. The National Assembly passed the enabling Act in May 1974, and the Allama Iqbal Open University (then named people's Open University) came into existence in June 1974. The chief executive of the university is the Vice-Chancellor who works under the direction of the executive council and the Academic council. The University has adopted a multi-media instructional system, the main components being (1) Printed materials (2) Non-Print materials like radio and television (3) Slides, audio cassettes, film charts, and leaflets (4) Guidance (5) Workshops (6) Courses assignments and their assessments and semester examinations.

Sri Lanka

Sri Lanka faced a major problem of training large numbers of teachers. To meet this demand the government set up three special institutions during the seventies. External Service Agency (ESA) to take over the extension programmes of the university, the institute of workers education to extend opportunities for university education beyond the normal undergraduate category and the Sri Lanka institute of Distance Education (SLIDE) to take over the extension services programmes of the Ceylon Technical College. This paved the way for the Open University of Sri Lanka which started functioning in 1980. Sri Lanka Government has close collaboration with the Swedish International Development Agency for their distance education programmes.

Thailand

Sukhothai Thammathirat Open University (STOU), Bangkok, has the distinction of having the largest Open University in the world. It was established in 1978. Though the STOU functions under the guidance of the Ministry of University Affairs, it has executive as the Rector. The two main Governing bodies of the university are the university council and the academic senate. To help the students who are scattered all over the country, the university has established a network of study centres. The university offers two types of programmes, viz., degree and non-degree. The STOU adopts a multi-media approach to instruction. Print material and radio and television broadcasting enable the students, to learn on their own without having to attend classes. In addition audio and video cassettes of various courses are available at the study centres. Tutorial and counseling sessions are also arranged at the study centres. It has adopted a grading system to assess the performance of students. Thus, the university serves a social purpose as well as an educational cause.

North America

Canada

Athabasca University is located in Alberta in Canada. It is dedicated to providing access to university education at the undergraduate level to adult Canadians who can not avail themselves of opportunities at more traditional universities. It was established in January 1970.

The President is the Chief Executive Officer and Vice-Chancellor of the university and reports to the governing council. The overall operation of the university is now divided into three functional areas (1) Academic (2) Finance (3) Administration and development. This university provides two types of the programmes: individualized study programme and university determined programme. The first one provides a framework within which students can plan and implement programmes and other one is administrative studies designed to meet the needs of people interested in furthering their education in the field of management. A typical Athabasca student first approaches the student service for pre-admission counselling. Students at Athabasca are assessed and given a percentage grade in a course on the basis of their performance in a set assignments/essays and examinations. Depending on the discipline and level, some courses have only one final examination.

Australia and the South Pacific Region Australia

There has been tremendous growth and consistent development of distance education in Australian. Distance Education courses had been started at all levels during the first decade of the twentieth century. Australia also has been active regional association of distance education called Australia and South Pacific External Association (ASPESA) to have a vigil over the functioning of various distance education centres. Some of the well known universities/ institutes providing distance education in Australia are Deakin, New England, Murdoch Queenland, the Royal Melbourne Institute of Technology and Gippsland Institute of Advanced Education.

New Zealand

New Zealand Technical Correspondence Institute's programmes are concerned with staff development, which consists of self-study materials combined with workshop. The New Zealand Technical Correspondence Institute (NZTCI) is a national organization that teaches vocational subjects at a tertiary level. All contact teachers in The New Zealand Technical Institutes other than NZTCI have teacher training entitlement of 12 weeks. NZTCI distance teachers, however, who train the students for the same national examinations, have an entitlement of only 6 weeks. The 200 hours of training for TCI teachers. As per the aim of NZTCI's its project trainees should have gained some insight into distance education, and have a better understanding of conditions that encourage adult learning. Under guidance from staff trainers and other experienced teachers, they would have gained practical experience in motivating and supporting their students, in preparing teaching materials, and in evaluating the work of students.

Europe

The Fern Universitate

The Fern Universitate was established by an act of Parliament of the State of North -Rhine West Phalia in November 1974. There are four types of students in the university like (a) full-time students, (b) part-time students, (c) guest students and (d) visiting students (Bartels, 1983). The Fern Universitate attaches great important to study centres. They are equipped with audio-visual media, projectors, recorders, reference library, photocopying machines. They offer information and pre-admission counselling prior to enrolment. In student evaluation, continuous assessment and term-end examinations are used. The university has plans to start several non-degree course programmes. The university has attracted students from different parts of Germany. Though the university derived its own system of distance education in which the emphasis is in printed materials and the learning packages, the university has broken new ground by instituting a distance education course namely essentials of distance education for distance educator. Print materials, tapes, videocassettes, computers, telephones, etc., are the medium being used for distance teaching.

Scotland

The Scotland Open Tech Development Unit has seen its expansion in many different areas through the Highlands and Islands in the North. As well as supplying Open Learning materials the unit has also been involved in the wider opportunities programme and the job training scheme. Many Open Learning systems are now using the modules as part of their offerings, either within existing schemes or creating new materials and schemes to lead to the SCOTVEC National Certificate, a system of equivalences between the City and Guilds and SCOTVEC allowing each body to provide endorsements to each other's certificates. TVEI developments have also included the action plan and Open Learning as part of the in-service training being carried out throughout the country. Open Learning has now become an integral part of the educational and training scene in Scotland. Open Learning enables training to be expanded beyond the confines of the traditional classroom and taken to the trainees at their place of work or home. Thus trainees can learn at a time, place and pace to suit the circumstances of themselves and their employers. This flexibility enable training to be undertaken as soon as it is needed and with minimum interruption to production.

Open Learning widens access to training and makes possible training which is more flexible and therefore, accessible to users. The flexibility of open learning methods means that training programmes can be more closely tailored to the particular needs of individuals and their circumstances. The cost effectiveness of open learning means that more people to undergo training and help to improve their job performance.

Sweden

The history of distance education in Sweden goes back to 1898 when H.S. Hermods started, a correspondence school. This school became one of the pioneering institution in the field of distance education in Europe. A correspondence school of the Swedish National Defense was also set up by 1966, with the merger of Norsk Korrespondenseshok Industright (NKI). Hermods, became the larger distance teaching institution of the world, started distance education programmes for university level courses in 1968 as a supplementary form of study, like the evening classes and local external courses.

United Kingdom

The establishment of the Open University at Milton in England in 1969, gave a new direction to the concept of distance education. Along with print mateials, it introduced audio and video materials and a system of personal guidance through contact centres for learners and their counselors. Although the combination of media varies in each course, the main emphasis is on printed text. Supplementary materials generally consists of broadcast notice to accompanying radio and television programmes, offprints, computer marked and tutor-marked assignments. Instructions are provided in the main printed text while radio or television broadcasts and related media and notes are supplemented.

In India

The following presentation provides an in-depth analysis of the situation for the purpose of gaining insight into the principle and practice of distance education in India. A correspondence programme for teachers, leading to a diploma, was introduced in India as early as 1955, but was subsequently discontinued. The first Arts degree was introduced by Delhi University in 1960 (Mullick, 1986). Correspondence teaching became more extensive in the following two decades. By 1982, thirty-three universities had introduced correspondence programmes. In most universities the number of students enrolled for study through correspondence is a small part of total enrollment, typically ranging from less than one per cent to just 11 per cent at Delhi. At two universities however, Tamil Nadu in the Southern Region, and Himachal Pradesh in the North Region, correspondence students comprised more than 20 per cent and 40 per cent respectively of total students enrollment. While problem of status and lack of adequate resources have been reported in various papers (Dutt, 1988), this substantive enrolment in correspondence courses at territory level shows the strong demand for distance education.

Dr. B.R Ambedkar Open University (BRAOU)

Andhra Pradesh Open University (APOU). It was

established in 1982 by an Act of Andhra Pradesh Government. Based on the report of Prof. G. Ram Reddy (1982) the Andhra Pradesh Legislative Assembly enacted the Bill and the university was inaugurated by H.E. Zail Singh, the then President of India on 20th August, 1982. The objective of this University is to provide equal educational opportunities in higher education for women, including house wives and adults and to provide flexibility with regard to eligibility for enrolment, age of entry, choice of courses, methods of learning, conduct of examinations and operations of the programmes. The student support services provided at the study center are, counselling, audio, video lessions, summer schools, practical sessions, library and information regarding to admission procedures, fees, examinations and counselling sessions etc. The students performance is assessed through continuous assessment through assignments and year end examinations.

Nalanda Open University

Nalanda Open University was established in 1987 with the objectives of promoting Open University and distance education systems in state. More specific objectives are:

- To provide educational opportunities to those who could not take up formal education and are still desirous to upgrade their education and interested in acquiring knowledge in various fields.
- To provide a second chance to those who had discontinued the formal education for various reasons including personal problems.
- To provide easy access to higher education to all and the disadvantaged in particular.
- To provide flexibility in matters of eligibility for enrolment, age of entry, choice of courses, methods

of learning, conduct of examination and operation of programmes.

- To offer degree and diploma courses and to make provision for research for advancement and dissemination of knowledge.
- To provide special facilities to groups like elderly people, in-service personnel, housewives, people living in remote areas, socially disadvantaged people of the society and all others who wish to upgrade their skill and acquire additional academic qualification through distance education.
- To lay emphasis on vocational as well as conventional courses, leading to award of degrees and certificates.

Vardhaman Mahaveer Open University

Vardhaman Mahaveer Open University was established in 1987, in the state of Rajasthan with the objectives of (1) Dissemination of knowledge through open and distance education (2) Making education accessible to all in a cost effective manner (3) To act as a resource center in the state for advancement of knowledge as well as research in the field of distance education (4) Have inter-locking with the national organizations specially with IGNOU (5) Development of effective technology based networking for spreading knowledge through the length and breadth of the state (6) To develop a flexible, convenient and attractive system of higher education. More than twenty programmes are offered in the open university.

Yashwantrao Chavan Maharashtra Open University

Yashwanthrao Chavan Maharashtra Open University (YCMOU) was established in 1989, had its antecedents in the Open Institution of the university of Poona under which a lot of preparatory work was done. The goal of the university is to become a "mass varsity". As such, it emphasizes vocational, technical and professional as well as general education programmes not only at the tertiary level but also at functional levels and outside the academic format, related to development and increased individual incomes. This university has planned courses in agriculture and horticulture for working farmers to study production processes with the help of specially written print materials audio-visual aids, two way communication between individual farmers and agricultural experts and contact sessions. For contact sessions, the university uses the concept of "Prayok Parivaars" i.e., a sort of extended "family" of "experiments" which enables producers/learners to set together to get/exchange ideas and benefit from each other's experience.

Madhya Pradesh Bhoj Open University

Madhya Pradesh Bhoj (Open) University was established in 1991 in Bhopal with the objectives of cost effective extension and promotion of quality education to reach the unreached, determination of standards and maintenance of quality in distance education, interventions of the well-being of the community, omnipresent education using emerging communication technologies and success through access. Twenty programmes are being offered in this university.

Dr. Babasaheb Ambedkar Open University

Dr. Babasaheb Ambedkar Open University was established in 1994 in the state of Gujarat with the objectives to advance and disseminate learning and knowledge by a diversity of means, including use of any communication technology, to provide opportunities for higher education to a large segment of the population, to promote the educational well being of the community, generally, to encourage the open university and distance education system in the educational pattern of the state. Under graduate and certificate programmes are offered in the open university.

Karnataka State Open University

Karnataka State Open University was established in 1996 in the state of Karnataka with the objectives of democratizing higher education by taking it to the doorsteps of the learners, promoting and developing distance education in India, offering need based academic programme by giving professional and vocational orientation to the courses, relaxed entry regulations, providing opportunities to study at one's own pace and convenience, providing opportunity to study from one's own chosen place. From certificate course to Ph.D. level programmes are offered in the university.

U.P. Rajashri Tandon Open University

U.P. Rajashri Tandon Open University was established in 1998 in the state of Uttar Pradesh with the following objectives

- To offer educational, training, research and extension programmes through open and distance learning for the development of the state.
- To provide education through distance education system to large segment of the population.
- To promote and advance the culture of the people of India and its human resources.
- Contribute to the improvement of the educational system by providing a non-formal channel complementary to the formal system and
- Strengthen and diversify the degree, diploma and certificate courses related to the needs of employment and necessary for building the economy of the country.

More than 36 programmes are offered in this open university.

Netaji Subhash Open University

Netaji Subhash Open University was established in 1997 in the state of West Bengal. The objectives of the university is to provide quality education in a flexible mode through the language of the state, i.e. Bengali, to make education affordable to disadvantaged, to provide facility for life-long education to intending learners, strive for upgradation of technology without compromising the basic values of the society, contribute to the development of the state and the nation and to motivate learners to strive for secular, scientific and democratic education. Under-graduate programmes are offered in the open university.

Tamil Nadu Open University

Tamil Nadu Open University (TNOU) was established in 2002 by Act No 27 of 2002 of Tamil Nadu Legislative Assembly, with the objectives of promoting open university and distance education systems in the educational scenario of the state. Specific objectives are:

- To provide an alternative, non-formal, cost effective medium for obtaining tertiary education to those who seek it.
- To provide a second chance to those who to discontinued the formal education due to personal problems.
- To promote easy access to good quality higher education to all and the disadvantaged, in particular, by delivering the same at their doorsteps.
- To provide an opportunity to those who are employed and wish to upgrade their knowledge and skills tailored to meet specific vocational and professional needs.

- To design an innovative system of university education that is not only flexibile with respect to entry criteria, but also with respect to what you learn, when to learn and how to learn.
- To design and provide local specific employment oriented programmes.

Communication Process - Role of Media

In distance education, teaching and learning take place between the teacher and distance learner through the process of didactic conversation and other means employed by the system. With the help of the latest communication technologies, dissemination of information can be done widely and effectively. Besides print media, other mass communication technologies like radio and television can also be used for quick transmission and wide coverage.

Abroad - Print Media

According to a survey made by Kember *et al.*, (1987) an overwhelming number of learners "consider academic support valuable in remedying problems with the study package. Meetings are more likely to be attended if they are lecture/ counsellor initiated and focus on learning difficulties or problems encountered in interpreting the learning package".

The summary of proceeding of the regional seminar on distance education held in Bangkok in 1986, gave importance to the instructional materials and it concluded with the statement

> "The quality of this material whether conveyed through the electronic media or through print, determines the success or failure of remote teaching; the quality and high standards of instruction determines the effectiveness of distance education. The well prepared materials not only instill

confidence in the students but prevent drop-out, and establish the status and reputation of distance teaching institutions".

Non-Print Media

Bates (1984) in his book, "The role of Technology in distance education" presents a collection of articles which stress that new technology aims at removing some of the disadvantages with the use of audio-visual media. It widens the range of available media. It is accessible, reduces cost and above all, it provides greater opportunities for revision, in-depth thinking, integration and interaction thus enabling students to develop skills through structured activities, practice and feedback.

Binder (1993) in his study "Measuring students attitudes towards television courses" states that the present series of investigations, taken together, provide a potentially useful and practical methodology for constructing an empirically based attitude evaluation instrument for televised courses The results of this project will encourage future tele-course evaluation researchers to begin structured assessments of students' reaction as the initial step in their overall evaluation efforts.

Dichanz *et al.*, (1992) conducted a study on the attitude of teachers towards media paradigms and interpretations as exemplified by television for school. Their study indicates that the implementation of television in instructions is an exception rather than the rule. A few teachers, most of whom have had better training in audio-visual education and are more open-minded towards television in their private lines, are motivated to include a television programme in their instruction to illustrate certain contents or simply to add variety to a lesson.

Garrison (1989) says that the increasing use of various kinds of technology in the distance teaching mode is leading to a more closely knit educational exchange between teachers and students, thus reducing the morphological differences between the distance and mainstream of education. Hence, he describes that the unique challenge that distance education faces in the changing technological scenario is how to utilize when contact between teachers and students is non-contiguous.

Norwegian distance educators discussed the use of media. A Conference on Distance Education in a technological society was held in 1983 at Sundvollen, Norway. The aim of the conference was both to give the participants a chance to familiarize themselves with new media and to discuss the need for and the function of each medium. One out of every twenty Norwegians enrolls each year as a student at a correspondence school and distance education is widely accepted as a part of the educational scene. The key word in such a discussion is accessibility, most Norwegins have a telephone, a television set, a radio and an audio cassette player. People are just beginning to buy video cassette players and home computers, cable television is on way in and new satellite facilities are accessible. The Norwegian Telecommunication Company is continually offering new services.

Paine (1985) states the role of new technology in open learning: -

- Can be used to produce conventional print based material more quickly and more effectively
- Can offer enhanced student support
- Can be used for pre-course, in-course and post-course testing
- Can help in the delivery of learning materials to the learner.

- Can improve the administrative system.

New technologies can help to overcome the distance between the learner and the providing institution whether this distance is a geographical or social. Television is particularly useful for experimental work because,

- Many experiments just cannot be performed at home, this is obviously true of this particular example, using a live rabbit's heart.
- Television through enlargement, editing and split screens, can enable students to see experimental work even more clearly than in a well-equipped university laboratory.
- Editing allows well-conducted experiments to take place saving the student's time.

Schramm (1977) considers televisions as one of the glamour boys of the media. It has attracted the attention of non-educators to instructional media. Instructional television not only transports the teachers, but could also bring with the teacher more elaborate illustrative material than any classroom teacher can possibly have at hand. Its main advantage is its accessibility. It reaches every home and it can be entertaining and attractive. It is therefore an important recruitment and motivation of students.

Schwittman (1982) studied the relation between time available for study and success at both the funk-kolley programmes by radio in Southern Germany and the courses at the Fern Universitat in North - Rhine west Falen. He claims that the time available for study is the only variable for predicting success or failure in a distance study programme. Further he says that a multimedia study package including visits to study centres, watching television programmes, utilization of course materials, doing assignments, helps one to forecast which element of the multi-media study package will be dropped first when one knows the relevance of each element towards the final examination and the amount of time available to the students.

Taylor (1992) observes that "Flexible access" is a key difference between the multimedia model and the deliberating model. For access to teaching through the deliberating model students must be present in a particular place (eg. Satellite campus, television studio, regional study center or an extremely well appointed home base) at a specific time in order to participate in the education process. "Flexible access" should clearly be regarded as a critical criterion in decision making associated with the provision of educational opportunities through distance education mode. Therefore he suggest that the limited funds available should be directed for enhancement of the multimedia model, through further development of those technologies, including computer-based learning and computer conferencing, which provide students with opportunities for both interaction and flexible access.

Videotex: the case of Fern Universitat

Videotex uses television and telephone in order to provide access to the computerized information. The Fern Universitat, Hagen is engaged in testing the application of videotex technique within its distance study system. This videotex programme provides information at two levels:

a. general information to the public about the Fern Universitat, and

b. specialized information to the learners.

The learner, by using his television set at home can avail himself of all those services which were so far available only in the study centres equipped with conventional display terminals. Moreover, all those facilities available to a learner who sits at a computer terminal in the university may be made available to the distance learners.

In India - Print Media

Davessar (1978) says that an important point to be kept in mind while preparing a unit of printed material is the length and the extent of the topic to be covered. Since usually a unit or lesson was assumed to be read by the student in a week's time, the teacher should carefully calculate the amount of matter, which one should ideally absorb in this time. Some lesson tend to be too lengthy, difficult to understand and grasped in one week's study by devoting, one or two hours a day. He stressed the need of knowing the extent to which a topic was to be covered and length of the lesson. Another important suggestion he made was about orienting the teachers of correspondence institutes to know their responsibilities towards the students and the society.

Paul (1978) describes the need for a close scrutiny of instructional material in view of the importance, which it holds in the scheme of correspondence education. He says, "It is not only the subject experts who form this team, but also the language experts, the media men and technical professional drawn from the printing trade are associated with the fabrication of lesson-unit of a given course".

According to Ramalingam (1994) printed materials are necessary and essential for effective distance teaching/learning in India because of limitations of non-print media like television, radio/video. In fact most of the distance education systems throughout the world both western and eastern are print based and likely to remain so.

Non-Print Media

According to Ananthasaynam *et al.*, (1989) the advances made in India in using communication technologies especially television, in recent years are satisfying. Further more

- modern media will help to disseminate information, more easily;
- media are also effective techniques for influencing the thinking of people.

Hemalata (1986) states that people belonging to scheduled tribe community of the southern districts of Rajasthan constituted tribal sub-plan area. In fact, it is difficult to electrify the tribal villages, for the habitation pattern of these villages, which are scattered. In such a situation electrification of these villages if not impossible, is very costly and difficult. Television it seems, would make the least entry in these villages. Owning a television set involves an expenditure which is almost beyond the meager budget of a poor tribal. Post office, yet another center of communication for distance education are few and far between in the tribal areas. Therefore she suggests that before we launch the programmes of distance education for weaker sections we must first prepare the infrastructure required for effective communication.

Teleconference/Interaction Communication Technology

Rao (1994) stress that traditional electronic media like radio, television, audio and video which are already being used in varying degrees at present by distance education institutions. While being effective in their own way, these media are all characterized by one outstanding limitation. It is in this context that the use of interactive technologies like teleconferencing become significant. In particular, audio teleconferencing can serve as an alternative to face-to-face counseling sessions at study centres or as a supplement to them for students located in far-flung areas or in the outer suburbs of big cities. In their case physical travel to the center would cost by way of both money and time. The techno-financial issues form the corner stone for developing audio teleconferencing systems in a big way for distance education purposes.

Reddy (1988) while describing the characteristics of distance education explains that the course system has tremendous flexibility with regard to the choice of the optional. Student is free to choose any optional which he likes; there is no rigid approach with regard to the combination of optional required to be taken by him. He further stresses the importance of communication technology such as radio, television, audio and video.

Satyapal (1979) observes that the biggest failure of the conventional system is that it is based on the principle of one way communication, where the teacher acts as a communicator and students as receiver. Hence there is hardly any scope for discussion, which is basically responsible for replacing existing educational system by a distance education channel.

Sharma (1994) states that at present provision of education to all is not possible within the formal schools or colleges and distance education is the only alternative to meet the educational requirements of the country. It is not possible to teach the students of remote areas, without using effective media. In the Indian context television has been acknowledged to be one of the most powerful mass communication media as more than 90 per cent of the areas of India has been covered by television. Television is good from the motivational, effectiveness and experimental point of view. Other media cannot compete with moving educational pictures and sound in bringing the 'world' into students living rooms at an affordable price.

Tyagi (1994) lays emphasis on teleconferencing as an electronic media which now-a-days is in use in the open learning institutions. It is an electronic media which brings together students located at different places to interact with their teacher who is at a different place through satellite based communication network. The technology of teleconferencing enhances the quality of interactive process and enables the students to contact the teacher from a distance easily. In this strategy the students get immediate feed back from the teacher and vice versa. In October 1993, Indira Gandhi National Open University, for the first time, in collaboration with the Indian Space Research Organisation (ISRO) conducted teleconferencing experiment to examine the effectiveness of satellite based interactive network system in distance education. It was one way video and two way audio. The ten regional centres of IGNOU were chosen as learning ends with three types of target groups and the academic counsellors.

The following three approaches were selected for this experiment.

- Orientation of academic counsellors
- Counselling of students
- Regular meeting of regional services division with the regional directors.

This novel experiment required a lot of preparation by the experts at the teaching end.

Distance Education has immense potential to impart knowledge in diverse areas. For instance famous actress Vaijayanthimala (Kungimam, Dec. 1982, p.70) has developed L.P. record on dance containing "Tala", "Song" and its grammar. Students desiring to learn the elements of the classic dance can use these L.P. record at home and practice as per the instructions.

Yadav (1993) points out that communication in the development of an Open Learning System network, has to be considered at the following levels.

- Within the Open Learning System network
- Interface of the Open Learning System network with its target student group and user industries.

At both these levels, the following may be taken as the "possible" means of communication:-

- Audio-telephone
- Audio-video including local area and wide-area computer networked teleconferencing, currently used in some western countries, and audio video tapes.
- Written material, and
- Personal contact.

The importance of written and personal contact cannot be undermined even though audio and video communication support could help information flow situation "within the Open Learning System network. Moreover, audio and audio-video communication could help to improve the interface of the Open Learning System with its target student group and user industries".

Student Support Services—Abroad-Study Centre

Sewart (1981) examined the role and need for study centres in distance education. He says that the existence of study centres can be attributed to an inability to develop the 'perfect' instructional package. From this perspective, Sewart terms study centers as the "dustbins" of distance education. He points out that the study centres provide the human element which is able to adopt the instructional package to the almost infinite variety of student needs.

Library

According to Noel (1992) Distance education has made tremendous progress in the past few decades, from a small correspondence to a modular package backed by audio visual aids and books loan provided by the correspondence colleges. Such a book loan service has gradually been developed into what we call as a mail or correspondence library. Perhaps, the term "external library is a better choice of words to describe such a special iibrary because it involves more than just a book loan through mail service. The external library is established to provide information for correspondence studies units and to help with any information enquiries an external student may have.

The external library will only be useful if the students know how to utilize the service; otherwise it is just a sheer waste of investment for a correspondence college to build up an impressive library. Tutor plays an important role in encouraging their respective students and advising them on how they can best make full use of the external library service provided to them.

Counsellor and Counselling

Kealey (1989) conducted a study on the distance learners who did not submit all their assignments, and when asked to give reasons for not doing so, the responses were:

- Lessons were too difficult to follow
- Unfavorable conditions for study
- Personal circumstances
- Other reasons

Miskiman (1983) states that a counsellor in many situations can only respond to the information offered by a student, which in the case of distance education is void of visual feedback information. Counselling is often limited in its ability to predict student's needs. This process is designed to enhance the predictive value of a counsellor's assessment of the distance learner's needs. One emphasis was on counselling techniques. The second emphasis concentrated on the identity of the distance learner. The difficulty with these two types of categorization is in their limited applicability to predict counseling needs of students. Although motivation has long been recognized as a vital aspect of performance level in education, much of what has been published simply states that intuitive thought is of little practical value. The application of this theory to the test of counselling distance student is advantageous for several reasons.

Perry (1976) while tracing the concept of evaluation of Open University staff says:

> "The concept of the open university evolved from the convergence of three major post-war educational trends. The first of these concerns development in provision for adult education, the second the growth of educational broadcasting and the third the political objective of promoting the spread of egalitarianism in education."

Distance education focuses on the educational needs of various groups of people like out-of-school youth, on the job people, farmers, teachers, housewives, and retried persons. Distance education system is flexible in its approach in the aspects of admission, course choices, methods of learning, time and pace of learning and examination.

Peters (1991) stresses the computerized counselling approaches of Fern Universitat. The small number of professional counsellors are not able to cope up with the situation due to large number of learners. The answers are put into the computer and are combined with a data bank of counselling texts that are written for each problem area. The computer letter is a very simple but effective procedure to a client situation. The use of such a system only make sense when there is much information on the university's side. The information given in the computer letter is meant to correct the "map" the client has of his future endeavor, or to respond in a positive, reinforcing way. Upto 89 per cent of clients have found such a letter helpful and would like to see this instrument of counseling continued.

Richard (1989) in his study "Staff attitude towards distance education at the university of Zambia" states that the University of Zambia operates an integrated system of distance education in which regular teaching staff teach both internal and external students. Although lecturers are contractually obliged to teach distance students they are mainly recruited to teach internal students. It is important, therefore, to determine their acceptance of correspondence teaching especially in a situation of staff shortages which result in high lecturer/student ratio.

Further, according to Richard the lecturers do not have enough time to carry out their correspondence teaching responsibilities. A small proportion of the respondents found it enjoyable. Also the majority thought it was fair for them to teach internal and external students. More so, to develop more positive attitude towards distance teaching, lecturers need some incentives and training especially in correspondence course writing.

Stinehart (1987) in her study indicates that more faculties perceived distance teaching. There were no significance differences in the way faculty willing to distance teaching and faculty unwilling to distance teaching. She perceived institutional support for distance instruction. Institutional support was not rated highly by the respondents. Cross tabulation suggested that opinions on distance teaching issues vary according to the telecommunications delivery mode used by the faculty member.

In India

Study Centre

Shukla (1994) views "study centres as a way to strengthen

students support services". He says that the smooth running of a study center very much depends upon the effective administrative and sound academy of that particular center. The close contacts between the study centers and regional centres and the students as well are a must. So, to maintain the contact, it is suggested that there should be regular visits of the officers of regional centres and frequent correspondence through posts. Assignments are evaluated at the study centres and consultants and tutors are easily available for this purpose at the study center.

Library

Devi (1994) discusses elaborately the role of "library" in the open education system, preparation of course material (print, audio, video etc.) and the network pattern followed by theses libraries. The contribution of libraries to education, both formal and non-formal and educational material can be seen as substantial and qualitative. The main emphasis is on open education students and their active participation. They need help from library and library staff. The saying "a university is as good as its library" appears so true in the context of open education.

Counselling/Personal Contact Programme (PCP)

Biswal (1979) in his study showed that all the institute of distance education had provision for personal contact programme. Even though the real purpose of personal contact programmes was not achieved to a large extent, most of the students who attended personal contact programme expressed positive opinion about the usefulness of the personal contact programme.

Murgan's (1994) analysis of the attendance of student for the counselling session conducted between January and June 1991 for various programmes reveals that attendance is moderate at 23 per cent. Various reasons can be attributed to the 'thin' attendance. One obvious reason is that the sessions are optional. Besides, distance learners being adults, their social obligations assume priority over education, notwithstanding the fact that they are motivated and have come to distance education by choice. Geographical inaccessibility to study centres would be another reason to be considered. The low attendance may also reflect on the quality of counseling sessions. A mere conduct of counseling sessions obviously does not guarantee quality.

Evaluation

Indu (1992) stresses that the formal and non-formal system consist of many subsystems. The underlying sprit behind the system of evaluation is to know the actual standard of examination, level of understanding, application and skill attained by the learner. Evaluation is essential to the whole system in the sense that it provides a feedback both to the teacher and taught how the system is delivering goods; whether or not the goals are being achieved. Generally the evaluation system comprises self-check exercises, periodic assignment, term end examinations and project work.

Jayagopal (1982) says that radio, television, and self study materials through distance education mode, help training of teachers who are serving the population located in far flung areas, punctuated by difficult terrain and inhospitable climate, which is a common feature in the third world countries. They can upgrade their qualification and maximize the use of resources available like the administrative personnel, technical personnel, curricular experts, instructional materials, forums for discussions through contact programmes and evaluation facilities. Inservice programmes for teacher/ counselors in the third world countries can be strong, provided they have the inputs of supervision, tuition, counselling with the aid of peripatetic field tutors, reinforced periodically by multimedia approaches.

Further he points out following weak points in the distance education programmes of India:

- Lack of competitive efficiency.
- Lack of co-ordination.
- Inadequate utilization of resources
- Lack of built-in monitoring and evaluation procedures.
- Lack of non-traditional programmes.
- Failure to improve contact programmes, home assignments and quality of lessons.
- Inadequate tutorial systems.
- Poor library services.
- Counselling sessions are not aimed at reducing number of dropouts.
- Lack of media as study center support.
- Lack of in service training to counsellors.

He concluded that the gap between planning and attainment may be due to lack of effective monitoring procedures. Effective monitoring is essential to attain the planned efficiency.

Race (1992) underlined the importance of assignments in distance education and said assignments

- Help learners prepare for formal examinations
- Give learners feedback comments on their work and develop their self-confidence.
- Give learners a measure of their successful work
- Form a basis for communication between learners and their tutors
- Motivate the learners to structure their studies in phased manner so as to complete the course successfully within the stipulated period

- Maintain and develop learners motivation and commitment to their studies.

Rao (1994) has discussed that assignments in distance education system provide the flexibility needed essentially to supplement the fixed academic input of print and other media. In fact, in distance education system often compulsory assignments alone form a contact point between the distance learner and the teacher and in developing the two way communication between them. Therefore, the methodology of evaluating these assignments should build sufficient interaction between the distance teacher and the learner.

Sathiyanarayana *et al.*, (1992) mention that students assignment holds a central position in distance education. Assignment constitutes considerable percentage of the final grade for many distance education courses in British Open University and 1GNOU. Assignments role in distance education may be summed up as follows:

- Provide student effective feedback through which students correct their progress
- Motivate the students
- Enable teachers to evaluate achievements during the course, so that they can help each students
- Provide the opportunity for tutors to motivate students by giving them encouragement and praise through written positive comments on students assignments.
- Activate the students' participation
- Provide students opportunity for application and transfer of their knowledge.
- Focus the student's attention on important learning objectives
- Develop methods for retaining knowledge and to practice writing

- provide opportunity for tutors to motivate the students by giving them encouragement and praise.
- Compel students to develop regularity of work.
- Create opportunities for contacts between teachers and students and thereby counteracting students feeling is isolation.

Saraswathi (1986) based on her research, indicates that the students are given extensive written materials but it is not supplemented by discussions on radio or television. The experts are not sure whether the students are entirely satisfied with the material given. The lectures in the contact programmes are repetition of written material but provide an opportunity for the students to clear their doubts. There are no adequate permanent members of staff for preparation of materials. Author' name and bibliography are not mentioned in the written materials and suggestions are not invited from the students about the materials. Sufficient number of assignments are given but there is no monitoring of corrections. Hence, she states that the courses have to be strengthened by introducing flexibility, diversity and innovation; above all, varied experiences have to be introduced.

Research, Staff Training and Development Abroad

The report of Commonwealth of Learning (COL) about the case studies on training, (COL 1990), concludes that training programmes should be

- suited to the needs of the institution
- available to all categories of staff
- suited to the experience of staff
- provide a sequence of training opportunities
- offer scope for carrier advancement and
- employ a variety of strategies.

A combination of distance mode methods and face-to-face mode methods should be adopted in training the staff and multi media should be used for training purposes.

Harthaway (1978) states that the completion rate of students enrolled in correspondence studies is low. At the same time evidence indicates that correspondence study may be regarded as a second form of education.

An analysis of collected data did not point to the differing attitudes towards learning by correspondence among groups studies. Adult students enrolled in correspondence study regarded it more positively than did principals of schools, where some students were enrolled in correspondence course. When compared to learning in the classroom, learning by correspondence was regarded more positively. Further, the attitude of distance learners were found to be significantly more positive than attitudes of students of formal education.

Heiler *et al.*, (1985) state that the development of the distance education programme related to building and construction courses for rural and isolated women is based on number of assumptions about distance education provision. They are:

- That courses can and should be developed for targeted groups, particularly women, in the same way as course are developed for apprentices and for the needs of industry and commerce.
- That in the development of distance education courses the experience of the target group in the face-to-face context should inform teaching and learning in the distance education context.
- That in organizing distance education courses, full provision should be made for those students who live at a distance from college centres.

- That access courses are an essential component of distance education system.
- That in recognition of the identity of the difficulty that writers, editors and teachers have in the shift to distance education modes, comprehensive staff development programmes are required for them.
- That the system must make provision in the development of distance education structures for maximum co-ordination flexibility.

Inglis's (1985) study is related to a major exploration of the development of learning attitudes by far North Queenland students. Attitudes which enhance learning by external students are promoted through the following strategies.

- By the provision of recognized adult learning strategies.
- By previous learning experiences, and
- By certain demographic factors.

The concept of promoting positive learning attitude through teaching for effective development is admittedly an ideal which carries with it tremendous strategic, economic and professional difficulties. Nevertheless, the evidence that exists in this small study is that students see teaching for effective development as an imperative.

Johnson (1983) concluded that the major reasons for the growth of distance education lay in the need for upgrading qualifications in response to technology change, the convenience of external study as opposed to its part-time equivalent and the changing status of women in our society. He believes his conclusions to be correct, but would add one more. That is external study has become respectable.

Lewis (1992) strongly advocates the competence-based

approach for staff development. He is very critical of the British Open University's top-down staff development approach and advocates a grassroot and participatory approach to build the competencies of staff.

Pal et. al., (1994) conducted a study entitled "a comparative study of the academic achievement motivation and attitude of students studying through correspondence and regular system of education at the graduate level". His study indicates that attitude of regular course students is more positive as compared to that of the mean attitude value for correspondence course students. That is the regular course students have more favowrable attitude towards education. It becomes evident that the students who pursue their studies through correspondence course are the students who had discontinued the regular studies, because of many reasons like, financial constrains and job etc. Besides this, attitude also plays an important role in choosing a particular course of study.

Africa

Rishante *et al.* (1985) conducted a study entitled "An investigation into the attitudes of Nigerian Academics towards a distance education innovation". The purpose of their study was to determine how faculty members in Nigerian universities perceive distance education innovation and how those perceptions relate to attitudes towards the innovation. Conclusions drawn on the basis of the above study include:

- There was no significant difference in the attitude towards National Open University of Nigeria across the contextual variables except for familiarity with distance education concepts.
- "Conventional system adequacy" and lack of distance education skills were the two major reasons for unwillingness to participate in the innovation.

- A discriminant analysis was performed on the above data, and it was found that 70 per cent of the respondents were correctly classified into the respective neutral and opposed attitude groups.

Thampson (1990) in his study explored the attitudes of post-secondary students who were negatively disposed towards correspondence based distance education programmes. The findings are students interaction increased with instructor as being the most important strategy for improving correspondence education. It would be effective to promote increased student to student interaction. Those educators who are responsible for the design and delivery of the distance education programmes should carefully examine the balance between resources committed to course-wise development and those committed to programme delivery. It is possible that in some cases disproportionately large share of resources were committed to courseware development.

Demiray's (1993) research study indicates that open education faculty has helped them to achieve their goals in this context. As another subject, it is well established that no education system will be successful and functional unless it renews itself according to the contemporary or social demands. The benefits gained by older adults by obtaining open university degree could be generalized as follows:

- To complete their educational development and strengthen their weak cognitive abilities.
- To gain self confidence
- To gain higher prestige in society
- To improve their income
- To have a more active leisure time
- To tackle the future more positively.

In India

Mani Gomathi (1982) in her critical study makes an attempt to utilize the technology of participant's evaluation of the correspondence programme. Her investigation indicates clearly that the relationship between 'lesson units', 'text book', 'contact seminar', 'instructors', 'radio broadcasts', and 'study centres', and achievement was significant whereas the relationship between 'response sheets', and the scheme of 'internal evaluation' was not significant. Also the attitude towards the correspondence course and achievement were significantly related.

Nath (1992) studied the academic problems faced by the students of the Andaman and Nicobar Islands studying through distance mode of teaching and learning system. Some of the problems printed out by him are:

- They don't get self-instructional materials and evaluated assignments in time.
- They could not attend the counselling sessions due to physical distance of study centers and lack of easy communication system.
- Study center timing not suitable
- No regular counselling sessions are arranged for some of the courses.
- Counselling session organized by the study center is not convenient for learning other subjects.

Jayagopal *et al.*, (1988) in their comparative study of learners of distance and formal education system presented an overall pattern; of grouping of characteristics levels of achievements; nature of distance and formal education system, etc. Open university system has not been properly used by the learners. Their investigation, pointed out that only learners of similar economic and cultural background avail the facility of distance education system in general and OUS in particular.

Jayashankar (1992) states that the quality of manpower that is inducted into the system of distance education decisively determines the quality of distance education itself. While other factors like the quality of study material prepared in print as well as on the cassettes stand aside, the efficacy of counselling, the existence of student services and the extensive use of modern communication technology do constitute vital inputs for maintaining quality in distance education. The efficacy of all these factors in turn depends upon the people handling the system. Therefore they emphasized the need for their attitude towards the system. Every care should be taken to providing necessary training and orientation to the people handling the system in order to make it more viable as an alternative to the conventional system.

Koul (1993) observes that "Workshops are one of the major means of imparting training in the various areas of distance education at present, and they will remain significant for quite some time to come, and therefore there is a need to make these workshops more purposeful by adopting a project approach".

According to Villi (1993) the reasons for drop-out of women learners from the Open University System are fear of failure in examinations; less retention power, marriage, heavy work load in the family, incurring more expenditure to the family, more office work, health problems of children and other family members, lack of contact with peer group, high standards of syllabus, high tuition fee, non-receipt of learning materials in time, etc.

Prasad (1994) states that staff training is an important input to maintain the quality of distance education system. The training of staff should be considered as an essential requirement of the distance education system because;

- Distance education is relatively a new field and most

of the staff to this new mode are from the formal system.

- Updating of existing knowledge and acquisition of new knowledge, new skills and positive attitudes are required for the job.
- Training build up the capabilities for taking higher responsibilities thus paving the way for career advancement.
- Trained staff contribute more and their performance add credit to the institution.
- Staff training is necessary for the adoption of new technologies.
- Staff training provides opportunities for self-development.

The commitment on the part of the staff coupled with effective leadership on distance education institutions can help to ensure the quality of the distance education system.

Rana's (1994) "A critical study of the distance education programmes in India in relation to role of IGNOU", study concludes that Distance Education Council (DEC) should be operational as soon as possible, so that distance education system will represent a distinct philosophy in educational technology. Such efforts will avoid duplication, save time and money. By this it can be ensured that a higher standard of quality education will be offered to students outside the reach of conventional centres of learning. Rana recommends that the study material should be translated into various languages. As the students do not get their print materials in time, the powers should be decentralized to the respective regional centres, for proper delivery. He concludes that large number of academic counsellors are not acquainted with the philosophy and communication methods of distance education and so should be given orientation programme.

An overall view of the concept and theory of distance education, Structure and Organization, Communication Process-role of Media, Supporting Service System Evaluation and Research, Staff training and Development were presented in this chapter.

3

Procedure of Investigation

Comprehensive picture of procedure of investigation related to data collection, sample size and statistical techniques employed to realise the objectives. They are presented below.

Statement of the Problem

The aim of the Open Learning System is to make higher education available to all those who wish to pursue higher studies as laid down in our Indian constitution under article No. 45, i.e. equalization of education opportunity for all. Moreover it is important for developing countries to provide functional education to all. This necessitates the utilization of all types of Open Learning structures and thereby equity can be achieved. In this context, it will be relevant to analyze the attitude of distance learners, which would facilitate implementing appropriate Open Learning Programmes. The problem focuses finally on the attitudinal dimensions of IGNOU learners, keeping the overall assumption that IGNOU functions as a major Open University System in India. Further it is deduced that the Open University System includes well defined objectives, regulations, courses, course completion requirements, time table and well defined clientele-faculty system. In this connection the following predictor and criterion variables are considered as relevant.

The Predictor (Independent) Variables

(1) Sex (2) Age (3) Religion (4) Community (5) Residence (6) Educational background of the respondent (7) Occupation of the respondent (8) Educational background of the parents (9) Parents' Occupation (10) Marital Status (11) Type of Family (12) Total monthly income (13) Study Centres (14) Categories of Programmes.

Criterion Variables

Attitude is the sole dependent variable

The Sub-Systems of the Open University

The following six major aspects of IGNOU Programmes have been identified for the study.

1. Admission Procedures
2. Printed Self-Instructional Materials
3. Non-Print Material—IGNOU Television Programmes
4. Study Centre/Library Facilities
5. Counsellors/Counselling Services
6. Evaluation: Assignment/Examinations

Keeping the predictor and criterion variables as constant, the following general and specific objectives as well as the hypotheses are formulated.

General Objectives

1. To study the socio-economic characteristics of the distance learners.
2. To study the attitude of the distance learners towards chosen subsystems of Open University.

Specific Objectives

1. To study the attitude of the distance learners in

different study centres towards the selected six aspects of IGNOU program.

2. To study the attitude of the distance learners pursuing different types of programs towards the selected six aspects.
3. To study the attitude of the distance learners towards admission procedures of IGNOU.
4. To study the attitude of the distance learners towards printed Self-Instructional Materials.
5. To study the attitude of the distance learners towards Non-Print with particular reference to television programs provided by IGNOU.
6. To study the attitude of the distance learners towards study center and Library facilities.
7. To study the attitude of the distance learners towards counsellors and counselling services.
8. To study the attitude of the distance learners towards Evaluation (Assignment and Examinations).

Hypotheses

The following null hypotheses have been postulated

*Six Aspects**

1. Admission Procedures
2. Printed Self-Instructional Materials
3. Non-Print Material - IGNOU Television Programmes
4. Study Centre/Library Facilities
5. Counsellors/Counselling Services
6. Evaluation: Assignment/Examinations

I. There will be no significant difference in the attitude of distance learners of different study centres towards the six aspects* of IGNOU programmes.

II. There will be no significant difference in the attitude of distance learners of different categories of programmes towards the six aspects* of IGNOU programmes.

III. There will be no significant difference in the attitude of distance learners of different age groups towards the six aspects* of IGNOU programmes.

IV. There will be no significant difference in the attitude of men and women learners towards the six aspects* of IGNOU programmes.

V. There will be no significant difference in the attitude of distance learners belonging to different religions towards the six aspects* of IGNOU programmes.

VI. There will be no significant difference in the attitude of distance learners belonging to different community towards the six aspects* of IGNOU programmes.

VII. There will be no significant difference in the attitude of distance learners of different locality towards the six aspects* of IGNOU programmes.

VIII. There will be no significant difference in the attitude of distance learners of different marital status towards the six aspects* of IGNOU programmes.

IX. There will be no significant difference in the attitude of distance learners having different educational background towards the six aspects* of IGNOU programmes.

X. There will be no significant difference in the attitude of distance learners of different occupation towards the six aspects* of IGNOU programmes.

XI. There will be no significant difference in the attitude of distance learners from different types of family towards the six aspects* of IGNOU programmes.

XII. There will be no significant relationship in the attitude of distance learners having parents with different educational background towards the six aspects* of IGNOU programmes.

XIII. There will be no significant relationship in the attitude of distance learners having parents with different occupation towards the six aspects* of IGNOU programmes.

XIV. There will be no significant difference in the attitude of distance learners of different income groups towards the six aspects* of IGNOU programmes.

Research Design

Considering the general and specific objectives, hypotheses, logistics, predictor and criterion variables and type of sample, the most appropriate design, viz., survey design has been selected for this study.

Research Tool

As per research design, for the purpose of data collection, a questionnaire was constructed. The questionnaire consisted of eight dimensions. The first dimension is related to the socio-economic status of the respondents with ten questions intended to elicit information relating to sex, age, religion, community, locality, educational background, occupation, type of family and income of the family.

The second dimension pertains to supporting systems provided to the open learners. This dimension includes the response related to receipt of self-instructional material, whether they have watched the television programme of Indira Gandhi National Open University, visited the study center/library and participated in the counselling sessions.

The third dimension pertains to admission procedures.

It aims to find out the attitude of distance learners towards age restriction, credit systems, and medium of instruction and the reason for joining the programmes also have been included in this questionnaire.

The fourth dimension of the tool consists of items regarding attitude of distance learners towards printed Self-Instructional Material (S.I.M.) their clarity, provision of charts and illustrations.

The fifth dimension consists of items regarding finding out the attitude of distance learners towards non-print media like IGNOU's television programmes, the suitability of telecasting time, motivational aspects of the programmes and whether there are repeated programmes to explain difficult units.

The sixth dimension consists of items to elicit information on the attitude of distance learners towards study center and library facilities provided by Indira Gandhi National Open University. The aspect covered relate to accessibility of study center, suitability of the study center working hours, availability of printed and non-print materials in the library.

The seventh dimension deals with the attitude of distance learners towards counsellors and counselling services provided by them, the counseling time, utility of counseling services, counsellors' experience, counselling approaches, and use of teaching aids.

The eighth dimension deals with the attitude of distance learners towards evaluation (assignments, project work and the examinations) system of Indira Gandhi National Open University.

The questionnaire was subjected to jury opinion. Based on the jury opinion some items were deleted and some others were modified and finally the questionnaire was designed with 10 items in the first dimension, 4 items in the second dimension and ten items each in the other 6 dimensions. For measuring the attitude levels of the distance learners towards several variables of the Open University Systems mentioned earlier, a five point Likert scale was constructed. In the Likert scale, the items or statements were followed by five response categories namely strongly agree, agree, undecided, disagree, and strongly disagree. The five possible responses were given weightage as 5-4-3-2-1. The score for the individual subject was the sum of all scores for the separate item in the scale.

Reliability and Validity

The tool consisted of 74 items. The same was subjected to testing in order to find out the reliability and validity. Along with reliability and validity the comprehensibility of the items were also tested. The tool was administered to 50 learners of the IGNOU study center located at New college in Chennai. Based on the study area and its level of understanding, difficult items were identified and the same were altered to suit the comprehension level of the subjects.

The reliability of the tool was assured by test-retest method for which it was administered to 50 IGNOU learners twice with an interval of one month. The reliability co-efficient of correlation is 0.782759. The co-efficient of correlation suggests that the test possesses reliability to a significant level. The research tool was validated by applying the content validity method. On the basis of the objectives of the study the concepts to be analysed were identified and the required number of items suited to each concept were identified and written. Thus the research tool was validated by applying the content validity method.

The face validity was established by requesting eight different experts to review the items and offer their comments.

On this basis, the questionnaire was reviewed and suitable modifications were made.

Sample

Four study centers of Indira Gandhi National Open University were selected for the study. The study centers selected for the study are New College in Chennai, Bishop Heber College in Truchirapalli, P.S.G. College of Arts and Science in Coimbatore and American College in Madurai which are in Tamil Nadu. The post - graduate structure of the Indira Gandhi National Open University programme in Tamil Nadu is such that only in the above four locations the study centres are available. Considering the importance and other logistics, the study has selected all the four study centres for chosing the sample. The universe represents the distance learners enrolled in Certificate, Diploma, Under Graduate, and Post Graduate (M.B.A.) programmes in the four study centres, during the year 1991. From the total population of 1453, enrolled at the study centres 50% (726) of the learners were selected as the sample.

TABLE 3.1

Sample Chosen

Study Centre	*Total Enrolment (1991)*	*Questionnaire mailed to 50% of the total*	*Receipt of Questionnaire*	*Percentage of received Questionnaires*
Coimbatore	388	194	45	23.19
Madurai	131	65	45	69.23
Tiruchirapalli	189	94	60	63.82
Chennai	745	373*	295	78.66

*Response was collected from the respondents in person.

Table No. 3.1 indicates the details of enrollment of distance learners. As per the design of the study 50 per cent of the sample was chosen by the stratified random sampling method. The details of the sample drawn were as follows

1. Certificate Programme (41)
2. Diploma Programme (78)
3. Under Graduate Programme (113)
4. Post-Graduate Programme (213) level distance learner

TABLE 3.2

Programme-wise Distribution of Sample

	Certificate		*Diploma*		*Under Graduate*		*Post Graduate*		*Sub Total*		*Total*
	M	*F*	*M*	*F*	*M*	*F*	*M*	*F*	*M*	*F*	
Coimbatore	2	—	5	1	6	1	24	6	37	8	45
Madurai	5	1	7	2	8	3	17	2	37	8	45
Tiruchirapalli	3	—	7	1	15	5	25	4	50	10	60
Chennai	19	11	47	8	60	16	130	5	256	39	295
Sub Total	29	12	66	12	89	24	196	17	380	65	
Total	**41**		**78**		**113**		**213**		**445**		**445**

M-Male, F-Female

Data Collection

The respondents' address were collected from the records and computer section of the regional office of Indira Gandhi National Open University with perior permission. The pre-tested questionnaire with self-addressed stamped envelopes were mailed to the respondents chosen from the three study centres of Coimbatore, Tiruchirapalli and Madurai. The Chennai (New College Study Centre) the filled in questionnaires was collected personally. After one month, reminders were sent to students from whom response was not received. In the ultimate analysis, out of the 726 questionnaires 445 were received after considerable persuasion.

Statistical Analysis

The value of mean scores and standard deviations were calculated from the data collected as per the research design. Analysis of variance (ANOVA) was adopted to test the significance of difference among the various groups. Further the '*t*' test was used to test the significance of difference between the mean gains at two levels. Correlation technique was employed to find out the relationship between the intervening variables and the dependent variables. The critical 'F' value and '*t*' value at 0.05 probability level were used to test the hypothesis.

4

Level of Utilization of Supportive Services

The present study based on the methodology described in the previous chapter, has been analyzed and the outcome are presented in this chapter.

For convenience sake the chapter on analysis is divided into three parts. The first and second part of the analysis deal with personalogical variables of distance learners, their attitude towards the six aspects- (1) Admission Procedures (2) Printed Self-Instructional Materials (3) Non-print materials-IGNOU Television programme (4) Study Center and Library and (5) Counsellor and Counselling (6) Evaluation: Assignments and Examinations) of IGNOU programmes. The third part of the analysis deals with the relationship between the selected variables.

The statistical techniques employed are analysis of variance (ANOVA), T-test and Correlation.

Utilising Supportive Services

The IGNOU provides self-instructional materials, Television programmes, Library facilities and Counselling session. The selected learners were requested to give their opinion about the level of utilizing the supporting service systems facilities.

The following tables provides details of the level of utilization of the support systems provided by IGNOU.

TABLE 4.1

Receipt of Self-Instructional Materials (SIM) by the IGNOU Learners

Time of Receipt Self-Instructional Materials	*Response (%)*
Immediately	26
Middle of the Course	49
End of the Course	14
Not at all	11

Table 4.1 indicates that 26 percent of the learners have received the SIM immediately after joining the course and 14 per cent of them expressed that they have received the SIM only at the end of the course. Forty nine per cent of the learners expressed that they have received the SIM only in the middle of the course, and 11 per cent stated that they have not received the SIM.

TABLE 4.2

Viewing IGNOU Television Programmes

Level of Viewing	*Response (%)*
Regularly	14
Often	43
Rarely	17
Not at all	26

From Table 4.2 it could be seen that 14 per cent of the learners are regularly viewing IGNOU programmes, 17 per cent of them rarely and 26 per cent of learners are not viewing

T.V. programmes. Forty three per cent of the learners are viewing the IGNOU programmes quite often.

TABLE 4.3

Periodical Visit to the Study Centre Library

Level of Visiting	*Response (%)*
Regularly	14
Often	26
Rarely	34
Not at all	26

From Table 4.3 indicates that 40 per cent of the IGNOU learners are visiting study centers and utilizing library facilities regularly whereas 60 per cent of them either rarely visit the library or do not visit.

TABLE 4.4

Attending Counselling Session

Attending Counselling Session	*Response (%)*
Regularly	23
Often	30
Rarely	23
Not at all	24

From Table 4.4 it is clearly visible that 23 per cent of the learners are regularly attending counselling sessions and 30 per cent of them often. On the whole in the sample size it is to be noted that 47 per cent of the learners do not attend counselling sessions at all.

Attitude of Distance Learners Towards IGNOU Programmes Whole Sample

TABLE 4.5

Mean and Standard Deviation of Attitude of the Sample Studied Towards the Six Aspects of IGNOU Programmes are Presented Below

Six aspects of IGNOU Program	*Max. Possible Score*	*Mean*	*Standard Deviation*
Admission Procedures	50	35.4	3.4
Self-Instructional Materials	50	38.2	2.7
Media-Television	50	35.1	2.9
Study Centre/Library	50	34.2	2.9
Counsellors/Counselling	50	42.3	3.1
Evaluation	50	43.5	3.2
Overall	**300**	**228.7**	**8.5**

PART-1

This part of the analysis deals with the attitude of distance learners at various study centers, programmes, age, religion, community, marital status and income groups. ANOVA was used to test the hypotheses.

Table 4.6 provides the mean and standard deviation(S.D.) for various attitude center wise and the same were compared using ANOVA. The ANOVA table related to above are as follows.

Major Hypothesis I

There is no significant difference in the attitude of the distance learners at different study centers towards the six aspects of IGNOU programmes.

TABLE 4.6

Attitude of Distance Learners in Various IGNOU Study Centers

Six aspects of IGNOU program	*Madras*		*Coimbatore*		*Tiruchirappalli*		*Madurai*	
	Mean	*S.D.*	*Mean*	*S.D.*	*Mean*	*S.D.*	*Mean*	*S.D.*
Admission Procedures	36.8	3.1	36.1	3.2	35.5	3.2	34.8	3.3
Self-Instructional Materials	39.9	2.6	39.6	2.5	37.8	2.4	37.5	2.6
Media-Television	36.2	2.8	36.0	2.6	35.3	2.7	34.9	2.8
Study Centre/Library	35.8	2.7	35.3	2.8	34.1	2.6	33.8	2.8
Counsellors/ Counselling	44.6	3.0	43.5	2.9	42.1	2.8	41.2	3.0
Evaluation	43.6	3.0	43.5	3.1	43.4	2.9	43.5	3.1
Overall	236.9	8.2	234.0	7.9	228.2	8.0	225.7	8.1

TABLE 4.7

Analysis Related to Different Centres and Six Aspects of IGNOU Programme

Source	*D.F.*	*S.S.*	*M.S.S.*	*Fc*	*Ft*
Between groups	3	118.4	372.8	5.31*	2.60
Error	441	30960.6	70.2		
Total	444	32079.0			

* Significant at 0.05 per cent level

From the Table 4.7 it is seen that the F value is significant at 0.05 per cent level and therefore the null hypothesis is rejected; i.e., there is significant difference in the attitude among the learners belonging to four groups towards the six aspects of IGNOU programmes.

The statistical value related to attitude is highest for learners belonging to Madras study center followed by Coimbatore, Tiruchirapalli and Madurai study centres.

Sub-Hypothesis 1 of the Major Hypothesis I

There will be no significant difference between attitude of distance learners at various study centres towards Admission Procedures of IGNOU.

TABLE 4.8

Analysis Related to Rtudy Centres and Admission Procedures

Source	*D.F.*	*S.S*	*M.S.S.*	*Fc*	*Ft*
Between groups	3	166.6	55.3	4.91*	2.60
Error	441	4966.0	11.3		
Total	**444**	**5132.6**			

*Significant at 0.05 per cent level.

From the Table 4.8 it is could be seen that the F value is significant at 0.05 per cent level and therefore the null hypothesis is rejected; i.e there is significant difference in the attitude of the learners belonging to four groups towards admission procedures of IGNOU.

The statistical value related to attitude is highest for learners belonging to Madras study center followed by Coimbatore, Tiruchirapalli and Madurai, study centres.

Sub-Hypothesis 2 of the Major Hypothesis I

There is no significant difference, between distance learners of various study centres towards self instruction material provided by IGNOU.

TABLE 4.9

Analysis Related to Study Centres and Printed Self-Instructional Material

Source	*D.F.*	*S.S.*	*M.S.S.*	*Fc*	*Ft*
Between groups	3	91.5	30.5	4.3*	2.60
Error	441	3145.3	7.1		
Total	**444**	**3236.8**			

* Significant at 0.05 per cent level.

From the Table 4.9 it is observed that the F value is significant at 0.05 per cent level and therefore the null hypothesis is rejected; i.e. there is significant difference in the attitude of the learners belonging to four groups towards self-instruction material provided by IGNOU.

The statistical value related to attitude is highest for learners belonging to madras study center followed by Coimbatore, Tiruchirapalli and Madurai.

Sub-Hypothesis 3 of the Major Hypothesis I

There will be no significant difference between attitude of distance learners of various study centres towards non-print material-Television programmes provided by IGNOU.

TABLE 4.10

Analysis Related to Study Centres and Non-Print Study Material

Source	*D.F.*	*S.S.*	*M.S.S.*	*Fc*	*Ft*
Between groups	3	116.2	38.7	4.72*	2.60
Error	441	3617.8	8.2		
Total	**444**	**3734.0**			

* Significant at 0.05 per cent level.

From the Table 4.10 it could be seen that the F value is significant at 0.05 per cent level and therefore the null hypothesis is rejected; i.e. there is significant difference in the attitude of learners belonging to four groups towards non-print materials—Television programmes provided by IGNOU.

The statistical value related to attitude is highest for learners belonging to Madras study center followed by Coimbatore, Tiruchirapalli and Madurai study centres.

Sub-Hypothesis 4 of the Major Hypothesis I

There will be no significant difference between attitude of distance learners at various study centres towards study centres and library facilities provided by IGNOU.

TABLE 4.11

Analysis Related to Study Centres and Library Facilities

Source	*D.F.*	*S.S.*	*M.S.S.*	*Fc*	*Ft*
Between groups	3	108.6	36.2	4.4*	2.60
Error	441	3625.4	8.2		
Total	**444**	**3734.0**			

* Significant at 0.05 per cent level.

As per Table 4.11 it is observed that the F value is significant at 0.05 per cent level and therefore the null hypothesis is rejected; i.e. there is significant difference in the attitude of the learners belonging to four groups towards study centres and library facilities provided by IGNOU.

The statistical value related to attitude is highest for learners belonging to Madras study center followed by Coimbatore, Tiruchirapalli and Madurai study centres.

Sub-Hypothesis 5 of the Major Hypothesis I

There will be no significant difference between attitude of distance learners at various study centres towards study centres and Counsellors/Counselling conducted by IGNOU.

TABLE 4.12

The Analysis Related to Study Centres and Counselors/ Counselling

Source	*D.F.*	*S.S.*	*M.S.S.*	*Fc*	*Ft*
Between groups	3	126.6	42.3	4.5*	2.60
Error	441	4142.2	9.4		
Total	**444**	**4266.8**			

* Significant at 0.05 per cent level.

As per Table 4.12 it is observed that the F value is significant at 0.05 per cent level and therefore the null hypothesis is rejected; i.e. there is significant difference in the attitude of the learners belonging to four groups towards Counselors/ Counselling conducted by IGNOU.

The statistical value related to attitude is highest for learners belonging to Madras study center followed by Coimbatore, Tiruchirapalli and Madurai study centres.

Sub-Hypothesis 6 of the Major Hypothesis I

There will be no significant difference between attitude of distance learners at various study centres towards Evaluation: Assignments and Examinations conducted by IGNOU.

TABLE 4.13

Analysis Related to Study Centres and Evaluation: Assignments and Examinations

Source	*D.F.*	*S.S.*	*M.S.S.*	*Fc*	*Ft*
Between groups	3	115.8	38.6	3.86*	2.60
Error	441	4430.8	10.0		
Total	444	4546.6			

* Significant at 0.05 per cent level.

From the Table 4.13 it could be seen that the F value is

significant at 0.05 per cent level and therefore the null hypothesis is rejected i.e. there is significant difference in the attitude of the learners belonging to four groups towards Evaluation: Assignments and Examinations conducted by IGNOU.

The statistical value related to attitude is the highest for learners belonging to Madras study center followed by Coimbatore, Madurai, and Tiruchirapalli study centres.

TABLE 4.14

Attitude of Distance Learners of Different Categories of Programmes Towards the Six Aspects of IGNOU Programmes

Six aspects of IGNOU program	*Certificate*		*Diploma*		*Under graduate*		*Post graduate*	
	Mean	*S.D.*	*Mean*	*S.D.*	*Mean*	*S.D.*	*Mean*	*S.D.*
Admission Procedures	33.9	3.2	34.8	3.3	36.5	3.3	37.1	3.6
Self-Instructional Materials	36.8	1.5	37.2	3.1	38.2	2.9	39.4	2.8
Media-Television	33.4	2.6	34.3	3.0	35.6	2.6	37.3	2.7
Study Centre/ Library	33.8	2.7	33.5	2.8	34.1	2.9	34.2	3.1
Counsellors/ Counselling	41.8	3.3	42.1	3.2	42.0	3.4	42.1	3.3
Evaluation	42.9	3.1	43.6	3.3	43.4	3.4	43.6	3.5
Overall	**222.6**	**7.2**	**225.5**	**8.6**	**229.8**	**8.8**	**233.7**	**9.2**

The attitudes towards the six aspects were compared programme wise. The Table 4.14 provides the mean and standard deviation value attitude to learners towards various programmes and the same were compared using ANOVA and the ANOVA tables are as follows.

Major Hypothesis 2

There will be is no significant difference in the attitude

of the distance learners of different programmes towards the six aspects of IGNOU programmes.

TABLE 4.15

Analysis Related to Categories of Programmes and Six Aspects

Source	*D.F.*	*S.S.*	*M.S.S.*	*Fc*	*Ft*
Between groups	3	1127.0	375.7	5.4*	2.60
Error	441	30952.0	70.2		
Total	**444**	**32079.0**			

* Significant at 0.05 per cent level.

From the Table 4.15 it is seen that the F value is significant at 0.05 per cent level and therefore the null hypothesis is rejected; i.e. there is significant difference in the attitude of the learners belonging to four groups towards the six aspects of IGNOU programmes.

The statistical value related to attitude is the highest for learners belonging to Post graduate programme followed by Under graduate, Diploma and Certificate Programmes.

Sub-Hypothesis 1 of the Major Hypothesis 2

There will be no significant difference between attitude of distance learners different programmes towards Admission procedures of IGNOU.

TABLE 4.16

Analysis Attitude of Distance Learners Related to Different Programmes Towards Admission Procedures

Source	*D.F.*	*S.S.*	*M.S.S.*	*Fc*	*Ft*
Between groups	3	158.4	52.8	4.67*	2.60
Error	441	4974.2	11.3		
Total	444	5132.6			

* Significant at 0.05 per cent level.

From the Table 4.16 it could be seen that the F value is significant at 0.05 per cent level and therefore the null hypothesis is rejected; i.e. there is significant difference in the attitude of the learners belonging to four groups towards Admission Procedures of IGNOU.

The statistical value related to attitude is the highest for learners belonging to Post graduate programme followed by Under graduate, Diploma and Certificate Programmes.

Sub-Hypothesis 2 of the Major Hypothesis 2

There is no significant difference between attitudes of distance learners of different programmes towards Self-Instruction Material provided by IGNOU.

TABLE 4.17

Analysis of Attitude of Distance Learners of Related to Different Categories of Programmes Towards Printed Self-Instruction Materials

Source	*D.F.*	*S.S.*	*M.S.S.*	*Fc*	*Ft*
Between groups	3	71.4	23.8	3.3*	2.60
Error	441	3165.4	7.2		
Total	444	3236.8			

*Significant at 0.05 per cent level.

From Table 4.17 it is observed the F value is significant at 0.05 per cent level and therefore the null hypothesis is rejected; i.e. there is significant difference in the attitude of the learners belonging to four groups towards Self- Instruction Material provided by IGNOU.

The statistical value related to attitude is the highest for learners belonging to Post graduate programme followed by Under graduate, Diploma and Certificate Programmes.

Sub-Hypothesis 3 of the Major Hypothesis 2

There will be no significant difference between attitude of distance learners of different programmes towards non-print material-Television programmes provided by IGNOU.

TABLE 4.18

Analysis of Attitude of Distance Learners Related to Different Programmes Towards Non-Print Study Materials

Source	*D.F.*	*S.S.*	*M.S.S.*	*Fc*	*Ft*
Between groups	3	111.0	37.0	4.51*	2.60
Error	441	3623.0	8.2		
Total	444	3734.0			

* Significant at 0.05 per cent level

As per Table 4.18 it could be seen that the F value is significant at 0.05 per cent level and therefore the null hypothesis is rejected; i.e. there is significant difference in the attitude of the learners belonging to four groups towards non-print materials—Television programmes provided by IGNOU.

The statistical value related to attitude is the highest for distance learners belonging to Post graduate programme followed by Under graduate, Diploma and Certificate Programmes.

Sub-Hypothesis 4 of the Major Hypothesis 2

There will be no significant difference between attitude of distance learners of different programmes towards study centres and library facilities provided by IGNOU.

As per Table 4.19 it is seen that the F value is not significant at 0.05 per cent level and therefore the null hypothesis is accepted; i.e. there is no significant difference in the attitude of the learners belonging to four groups towards study centres and library facilities provided by IGNOU.

TABLE 4.19

Analysis of Attitude of Distance Learners of Different Categories Towards Programmes and Study Centres and Library Facilities

Source	*D.F.*	*S.S.*	*M.S.S.*	*Fc*	*Ft*
Between groups	3	54.7	18.2	2.2	2.60
Error	441	3679.3	8.2		
Total	444	3734.0			

Sub-Hypothesis 5 of the Major Hypothesis 2

There will be no significant difference between attitude of distance learners of different programmes towards Counsellors/Counselling conducted by IGNOU.

TABLE 4.20

Analysis Related to Study Centres and Counsellers/Counselling

Source	*D.F.*	*S.S.*	*M.S.S.*	*Fc*	*Ft*
Between groups	3	36.5	12.1	1.26	2.60
Error	441	4230.3	9.6		
Total	444	4266.8			

As per Table 4.20 it could be seen that the F value is not significant at 0.05 per cent level and therefore the null hypothesis is accepted; i.e. there is no significant difference in the attitude of the learners belonging to four groups towards Counsellors/Counselling conducted by IGNOU.

Sub-Hypothesis 6 of the Major Hypothesis 2

There will be no significant difference between attitude of distance learners of different programmes towards Evaluation: Assignments and Examinations conducted by IGNOU.

TABLE 4.21

Analysis of Attitudes of Distance Learners of Different Categories of Programmes Towards Evaluation: Assignments and Examinations

Source	*D.F.*	*S.S.*	*M.S.S.*	*Fc*	*Ft*
Between groups	3	115.8	38.6	3.86*	2.60
Error	441	4430.8	10.0		
Total	444	4546.6			

* Significant at 0.05 per cent level

From the Table 4.21 it is deduced that the F value is significant at 0.05 per cent level and therefore the null hypothesis is rejected; i.e. there is significant difference in the attitude of the learners belonging to four groups towards evaluation conducted by IGNOU.

TABLE 4.22

Attitude of Distance Learners of Various Age Groups

Six aspects of IGNOU program	*16-25*		*26-25*		*36-45*		*46 & above*	
	Mean	*S.D.*	*Mean*	*S.D.*	*Mean*	*S.D.*	*Mean*	*S.D.*
Admission Procedures	34.8	2.9	34.9	2.9	35.5	3.1	36.2	3.0
Self-Instructional Materials	39.6	2.4	29.2	2.6	37.6	2.5	37.2	2.5
Media-Television	36.7	2.6	35.3	2.5	34.8	2.6	34.6	2.7
Study Centre/Library	35.8	2.5	35.0	2.7	33.8	2.6	33.4	2.5
Counsellors/Counselling	43.6	2.7	42.8	2.8	41.7	2.9	41.2	2.7
Evaluation	44.8	2.8	44.1	2.9	43.1	3.0	42.5	2.9
Overall	**235.3**	**7.8**	**222.3**	**8.1**	**226.5**	**8.2**	**225.1**	**8.1**

The statistical value related to attitude is highest for learners belonging to Post graduate programme followed by Under graduate, Diploma and Certificate Programmes.

The attitude of distance learners towards various dimensions of Open University were compared age-wise. The Table 4.22 provides the mean and standard deviation value of attitude of distance learners belonging to various age groups and the same were compared using ANOVA. The ANOVA tables are as follows:

Major Hypothesis 3

There will be is no significant difference in the attitude of the distance learners of different age groups towards six aspects of IGNOU programmes

TABLE 4.23

Analysis Related to Age and Attitude Towards the Six Aspects of IGNOU Programmes

Source	*D.F.*	*S.S.*	*M.S.S.*	*Fc*	*Ft*
Between groups	3	1314.9	438.3	6.3*	2.60
Error	441	30764.1	69.8		
Total	444	32079.0			

* Significant at 0.05 per cent level.

From the Table 4.23 it is seen that the F value is significant at 0.05 per cent level and therefore the null hypothesis is rejected; i.e. there is significant difference in the attitude of the learners belonging to various age groups towards the six aspects of IGNOU programmes.

The statistical value related to attitude is the highest for learners belonging to the age group 16-25 followed by the 26-35, 36-45 and 46 and above.

Sub-Hypothesis 1 of the Major Hypothesis 3

There will be no significant difference between attitude of distance learners of various age groups towards Admission procedures of IGNOU.

TABLE 4.24

Analysis of Attitude of Distance Learners Related to Age and Attitude Towards Admission Procedures of IGNOU

Source	*D.F.*	*S.S.*	*M.S.S.*	*Fc*	*Ft*
Between groups	3	162.8	54.2	4.80*	2.60
Error	441	4969.8	11.3		
Total	444	5132.6			

* Significant at 0.05 per cent level.

From the Table 4.24 it could be seen that the F value is significant at 0.05 per cent level and therefore the null hypothesis is rejected; i.e. there is significant difference in the attitude of the learners belonging to various age groups towards admission procedures of IGNOU.

The statistical value related to attitude is the highest for learners belonging to the age group of 46 and above followed by 36-45, 26-35, and 16-25.

Sub-Hypothesis 2 of the Major Hypothesis 3

There will be no significant difference between attitudes of distance learners of various age groups towards six aspects of IGNOU programmes.

As per Table 4.25 it is observed the F value is significant at 0.05 per cent level and therefore the null hypothesis is rejected; i.e. there is significant difference among the learners belonging to various age groups towards Self- Instruction Material provided by IGNOU.

TABLE 4.25

Analysis of Age and Attitude of Distance Learners of Different Categories of Programmes Towards Printed Self-Instruction Materials

Source	*D.F.*	*S.S.*	*M.S.S.*	*Fc*	*Ft*
Between groups	3	101.3	33.8	4.8*	2.60
Error	441	3135.5	7.1		
Total	**444**	**3236.8**			

* Significant at 0.05 per cent level.

The statistical value related to attitude is the highest for learners belonging to the age group of 16-25 followed by the 36-45 and 46 and above and 26-35 age groups.

Sub-Hypothesis 3 of the Major Hypothesis 3

There will be no significant difference between attitude of distance learners of various age groups towards non-print material-Television programmes provided by IGNOU.

TABLE 4.26

Analysis Related to Age and Attitude Towards Non-Print Study Materials

Source	*D.F.*	*S.S.*	*M.S.S.*	*Fc*	*Ft*
Between groups	3	114.2	38.7	4.7*	2.60
Error	441	3617.8	8.2		
Total	444	3734.0			

*Significant at 0.05 per cent level.

From the Table 4.26 it could be seen that the F value is significant at 0.05 per cent level and therefore the null hypothesis is rejected; i.e. there is significant difference in the attitude of the learners belonging various age groups towards non-print materials -Television programmes provided by IGNOU.

The statistical value related to attitude is the highest for distance learners belonging to the age group of 16-25 age group followed by the 26-35, 36-45 and 46 and above.

Sub-Hypothesis 4 of the Major Hypothesis 3

There will be no significant difference between attitude of distance learners of various age groups towards study centres and library facilities provided by IGNOU.

TABLE 4.27

Analysis of Age and Attitude Towards Study Centres/Library Facilities

Source	*D.F.*	*S.S.*	*M.S.S.*	*Fc*	*Ft*
Between groups	3	88.3	29.4	3.55*	2.60
Error	441	3645.7	8.3		
Total	**444**	**3734.0**			

*Significant at 0.05 per cent level

From the Table 4.27 it could be seen that the F value is significant at 0.05 per cent level and therefore the null hypothesis is rejected; i.e. there is significant difference in the attitude of the learners belonging various age groups towards Study centres/Library facilities provided by IGNOU.

The statistical value related to attitude is the highest for distance learners belonging to the age group of 16-25 age group followed by the 26-35, 46 and above and 36-45.

Sub-Hypothesis 5 of the Major Hypothesis 3

There will be no significant difference between attitude of distance learners of various age groups towards Counsellors/Counselling conducted by IGNOU.

TABLE 4.28

Analysis Related to Study Centres and Counsellers/Counselling

Source	*D.F.*	*S.S.*	*M.S.S.*	*Fc*	*Ft*
Between groups	3	108.4	36.2	8.85*	2.60
Error	441	4158.2	9.4		
Total	**444**	**4266.8**			

*Significant at 0.05 per cent level.

From the Table 4.28 it could be seen that the F value is significant at 0.05 per cent level and therefore the null hypothesis is rejected; i.e. there is significant difference in the attitude of the learners belonging various age groups in the attitude towards Counsellors/Counselling conducted by IGNOU.

The statistical value related to attitude is the highest for distance learners belonging to the age group of 16-25 age group followed by the 26-35, 36-45 and 46 and above.

Sub-Hypothesis 6 of the Major Hypothesis 3

There will be no significant difference between the attitude of distance learners of various age groups towards evaluation: Assignments/Examinations conducted by IGNOU.

TABLE 4.29

Analysis Related to Age and Attitudes Towards Evaluation: Assignments and Examinations

Source	*D.F.*	*S.S.*	*M.S.S.*	*Fc*	*Ft*
Between groups	3	166.8	38.9	3.89*	2.60
Error	441	4429.8	10.0		
Total	**444**	**4546.6**			

* Significant at 0.05 per cent level.

From the Table 4.29 it could be seen that the F value is significant at 0.05 per cent level and therefore the null hypothesis is rejected; i.e. there is significant difference in the attitude of the learners belonging to various age groups in the attitude towards Evaluation: Assignments/Examinations conducted by IGNOU.

The statistical value related to attitude is highest for learners belonging to the age group of 16-25 age group followed by the 26-35, 36-45 and 46 and above.

TABLE 4.30

Attitude of Distance Learners Belonging to Different Religions Towards the Six Aspects

Six aspects of IGNOU program	*Hindu*		*Muslim*		*Christan*		*Others*	
	Mean	*S.D.*	*Mean*	*S.D.*	*Mean*	*S.D.*	*Mean*	*S.D.*
Admission Procedures	35.9	3.0	35.3	2.9	35.8	3.1	35.4	3.2
Self-Instructional Materials	38.3	2.3	37.8	2.4	38.0	2.3	37.7	2.5
Media-Television	35.3	2.5	35.0	2.6	35.1	2.3	34.9	2.4
Study Centre/Library	34.2	2.4	34.0	2.7	34.1	2.5	33.9	2.
Counsellors/ Counselling	41.9	2.7	42.0	2.5	42.3	2.9	41.8	2.6
Evaluation	43.2	2.8	43.4	2.9	43.5	2.7	43.1	3.0
Overall	**228.8**	**8.1**	**227.5**	**7.9**	**228.7**	**8.3**	**226.8**	**8.2**

The attitude of distance learners towards various dimensions were compared religion wise. Table 4.30 gives the mean and standard deviation (S.D) for various attitudes religion wise which were compared using ANOVA. The ANOVA tables are as follows.

Major Hypothesis 4

There will be is no significant difference between the attitude of the distance learners belonging to different religions towards six aspects of IGNOU programmes.

TABLE 4.31

Analysis Related to Religions and Six Aspects of IGNOU Programmes

Source	*D.F.*	*S.S.*	*M.S.S.*	*Fc*	*Ft*
Between groups	3	664.7	221.6	3.11*	2.60
Error	441	31414.3	71.2		
Total	**444**	**32079.0**			

* Significant at 0.05 per cent level.

From the Table 4.31 it is seen that the F value is significant at 0.05 per cent level and therefore the null hypothesis is rejected; i.e. there is significant difference in the attitude of the learners belonging to the four religious groups towards the six aspects of IGNOU programmes.

The statistical value related to the attitude is the highest for learners belonging to Hindu followed by the Christian, Muslim and other religions.

TABLE 4.32

Analysis Attitude of Distance Learners of Different Religions Towards Admission Procedures of IGNOU

Source	*D.F.*	*S.S.*	*M.S.S.*	*Fc*	*Ft*
Between groups	3	68.2	22.7	1.97	2.60
Error	441	5064.4	4.5		
Total	**444**	**5132.6**			

Sub-Hypothesis 1 of the Major Hypothesis 4

There will be no significant difference between attitude

of distance learners of various age groups towards Admission procedures of IGNOU.

As per the Table 4.32 it could be seen that the F value is not significant at 0.05 per cent level and therefore the null hypothesis is accepted; i.e. there is significant difference in the attitude of the learners belonging to the four religious groups towards the admission procedures of IGNOU.

Sub-Hypothesis 2 of the Major Hypothesis 4

There will be no significant difference between attitudes of distance learners of various religions towards Self-Instruction Materials provided by IGNOU.

TABLE 4.33

Analysis Related to Religion and the Attitude Towards Printed Self-Instruction Materials

Source	*D.F.*	*S.S.*	*M.S.S.*	*Fc*	*Ft*
Between groups	3	44.5	14.8	2.1	2.60
Error	441	3192.3	7.2		
Total	**444**	**3236.8**			

From the Table 4.33 it is observed that the F value is not significant at 0.05 per cent level and therefore the null hypothesis is accepted; i.e. there is no significant difference in the attitude of the learners belonging to the four religious groups towards Self- Instruction Material provided by IGNOU.

Sub-Hypothesis 3 of the Major Hypothesis 4

There will be no significant difference between attitude of distance learners of various religions towards non-print material-Television programmes provided by IGNOU.

From the Table 4.34 it could be seen that the F value is not significant at 0.05 per cent level and therefore the null hypothesis is accepted; i.e. there is no significant difference in the attitude of the learners belonging to the four religious in the attitude towards non-print materials - Television programmes provided by IGNOU.

TABLE 4.34

Analysis Related to Religions and Attitude Towards Non-Print Study Materials

Source	*D.F.*	*S.S.*	*M.S.S.*	*Fc*	*Ft*
Between groups	3	114.2	38.7	4.7*	2.60
Error	441	3617.8	8.2		
Total	**444**	**3734.0**			

Sub-Hypothesis 4 of the Major Hypothesis 4

There will be no significant difference between attitude of distance learners of different religions towards study centres and library facilities provided by IGNOU

TABLE 4.35

Analysis Related to Religions and Attitude Towards Study Centres/Library Facilities

Source	*D.F.*	*S.S.*	*M.S.S.*	*Fc*	*Ft*
Between groups	3	45.4	15.1	1.8	2.60
Error	441	3688.6	8.4		
Total	**444**	**3734.0**			

From the Table 4.35 it could be seen that the F value is not significant at 0.05 per cent level and therefore the null hypothesis is accepted; i.e. there is no significant difference in the attitude of the learners belonging to the four religion groups towards study centers/library facilities provided by IGNOU.

Sub-Hypothesis 5 of the Major Hypothesis 4

There will be no significant difference between attitude

of distance learners of different religions towards Counsellors/ Counselling conducted by IGNOU.

TABLE 4.36

Analysis Related to Religions and Counsellers/Counselling

Source	*D.F.*	*S.S.*	*M.S.S.*	*Fc*	*Ft*
Between groups	3	55.7	18.6	1.9	2.60
Error	441	4211.1	9.5		
Total	**444**	**4266.8**			

From the Table 4.36 it could be seen that the F value is not significant at 0.05 per cent level and therefore the null hypothesis is accepted; i.e. there is no significant difference in the attitude of the learners belonging to the four religious groups towards Counsellors/Counselling conducted by IGNOU.

Sub-Hypothesis 6 of the Major Hypothesis 4

There will be no significant difference between the attitude of distance learners of different religions towards evaluation: Assignments/Examinations conducted by IGNOU.

TABLE 4.37

Analysis Related to Religions and Attitudes Towards Evaluation: Assignments and Examinations

Source	*D.F.*	*S.S.*	*M.S.S.*	*Fc*	*Ft*
Between groups	3	116.8	38.9	3.89*	2.60
Error	441	4429.8	10.0		
Total	**444**	**4544.6**			

From the Table 4.37 it could be seen that the F value is not significant at 0.05 per cent level and therefore the null hypothesis is accepted; i.e. there is no significant difference in the attitude of the learners belonging to the four religious groups towards Evaluation: Assignments/Examinations conducted by IGNOU.

TABLE 4.38

Attitude of Distance Learners of Various Communities

Six aspects of IGNOU program	*S.C.*		*S.T.*		*B.C.*		*M.B.C.*		*F.C.*	
	Mean	*S.D.*	*Mean*	*S.D.*	*Mean*	*S.D.*	*Mean*	*S.D.*	*Mean*	*S.D.*
Admission Procedures	36.8	3.1	36.9	3.0	35.5	2.9	35.9	3.0	34.5	3.1
Self-Instructional Materials	37.1	2.3	37.4	2.4	38.5	2.3	37.8	2.4	39.2	2.5
Media-Television	34.8	2.5	34.6	2.6	35.6	2.8	34.9	2.7	36.2	2.6
Study Centre/Library	35.2	2.6	35.3	2.7	34.8	2.6	33.6	2.7	33.8	2.5
Counsellors/ Counselling	42.6	2.8	42.8	2.9	41.8	3.0	41.9	2.9	41.6	2.7
Evaluation	43.1	2.9	43.0	2.6	43.4	3.0	43.2	3.1	43.5	2.9
Overall	**229.6**	**7.8**	**230.0**	**7.9**	**229.6**	**8.2**	**227.3**	**8.1**	**228.8**	**8.0**

S.C. - Scheduled Castes; S.T. - Scheduled Tribes; B.C. - Backward Class; M.B.C. - Most Backward Class; F.C. - Forward Communities.

The attitude of distance learners towards the six aspects of IGNOU programmes were compared community wise. The Table 4.38 gives the mean and standard deviation (S.D) for the various attitudes value towards the various aspects of IGNOU programmes of learners community wise. They were compared using ANOVA. The ANOVA tables are as follows:

Major Hypothesis 5

There will be is no significant difference between the attitude of the distance learners belonging to different communities towards six aspects of IGNOU programmes.

TABLE 4.39

Analysis Related to Community and Six Aspects

Source	*D.F.*	*S.S.*	*M.S.S.*	*Fc*	*Ft*
Between groups	4	953.7	238.4	3.4*	2.60
Error	440	31125.3	70.7		
Total	**444**	**32079.0**			

* Significant at 0.05 per cent level.

From the Table 4.39 it is seen that the F value is significant at 0.05 per cent level and therefore the null hypothesis is rejected; i.e. there is significant difference in the attitude of the learners belonging to the five community groups towards the six aspects of IGNOU programmes.

The statistical value related to the attitude is the highest for learners belonging to scheduled tribes followed by the Scheduled caste, Backward, Forward and Most Backward communities.

Sub-Hypothesis 1 of the Major Hypothesis 5

There will be no significant difference between attitude of distance learners of various community groups towards admission procedures of IGNOU.

TABLE 4.40

Analysis Attitude of Distance Learners to Community and Attitudes Towards Admission Procedures of IGNOU

Source	*D.F.*	*S.S.*	*M.S.S.*	*Fc*	*Ft*
Between groups	4	171.1	42.0	3.78*	2.37
Error	440	4961.5	11.3		
Total	**444**	**5132.6**			

From the Table 4.40 it could be seen that the F value is significant at 0.05 per cent level and therefore the null hypothesis is rejected; i.e. there is significant difference in the attitude of the learners belonging to the five community groups towards admission procedures of IGNOU.

The statistical value related to the attitude is the highest for the learners belonging to Scheduled tribe learners followed by Scheduled caste, Most Backward, Backward, and Forward communities.

Sub-Hypothesis 2 of the Major Hypothesis 5

There will be no significant difference between attitudes of distance learners of Different communities towards Self-Instruction Materials provided by IGNOU.

TABLE 4.41

Analysis Related to the Religion and the Attitude Towards the Printed Self- Instruction Materials

Source	*D.F.*	*S.S.*	*M.S.S.*	*Fc*	*Ft*
Between groups	4	118.1	29.5	4.1*	2.37
Error	440	3118.7	7.1		
Total	**444**	**3236.8**			

* Significant at 0.05 per cent level.

From the Table 4.41 it is observed the F value is significant at 0.05 per cent level and therefore the null hypothesis is rejected; i.e. there is significant difference in the attitude of the learners belonging to the five community groups towards Self- Instruction Material provided by IGNOU.

The statistical value related to the attitude is the highest for the learners belonging to Forward community followed by the Backward, Most Backward communities, Scheduled tribes and Scheduled caste communities.

Sub-Hypothesis 3 of the Major Hypothesis 5

There will be no significant difference between attitude

of distance learners of various communities towards non-print material-Television programmes provided by IGNOU.

TABLE 4.42

Analysis Related to the Community and the Attitude Towards Non-print Study Materials

Source	*D.F.*	*S.S.*	*M.S.S.*	*Fc*	*Ft*
Between groups	4	122.8	30.7	3.74*	2.37
Error	440	3611.2	8.2		
Total	444	3734.0			

* Significant at 0.05 per cent level.

From the Table 4.42 it could be seen that the F value is significant at 0.05 per cent level and therefore the null hypothesis is rejected; i.e. there is significant difference in the attitude of the learners belonging to the five community groups towards non-print materials - Television programmes provided by IGNOU.

The statistical value related to the attitude is the highest for the learners belonging to Forward community followed by the Backward, Most Backward, Scheduled tribes and Scheduled caste communities.

Sub-Hypothesis 4 of the Major Hypothesis 5

There will be no significant difference between attitude of distance learners of various communities towards study centres and library facilities provided by IGNOU.

From the Table 4.43 it could be seen that the F value is significant at 0.05 per cent level and therefore the null hypothesis is rejected; i.e. there is significant difference in the attitude of the learners belonging to the five community groups towards study centers/library facilities provided by IGNOU.

TABLE 4.43

Analysis Related to Community and Attitude Towards Study Centres/Library Facilities

Source	*D.F.*	*S.S.*	*M.S.S.*	*Fc*	*Ft*
Between groups	4	132.0	33.0	4.0*	2.37
Error	440	3602.0	8.2		
Total	**444**	**3734.0**			

* Significant at 0.05 per cent level.

The statistical value related to the attitude is the highest for the learners belonging to Scheduled tribes followed by the Scheduled caste, Backward, Most Backward and Forward communities.

Sub-Hypothesis 5 of the Major Hypothesis 5

There will be no significant difference between attitude of distance learners of various communities towards Counsellors/Counselling conducted by IGNOU.

TABLE 4.44

Analysis Related to Community and Attitudes Towards Counsellers/Counselling

Source	*D.F.*	*S.S.*	*M.S.S.*	*Fc*	*Ft*
Between groups	4	158.6	372.8	5.31*	2.60
Error	440	4108.2	9.3		
Total	**444**	**4266.8**			

* Significant at 0.05 per cent level.

From the Table 4.44 it could be seen that the F value is significant at 0.05 per cent level and therefore the null hypothesis is rejected; i.e. there is significant difference in the attitude of the learners belonging to the five community groups towards Counsellors/Counselling conducted by IGNOU.

The statistical value related to the attitude is the highest for the learners belonging to the Scheduled tribes followed by the Scheduled caste, Most Backward, Backward and Forward communities.

Sub-Hypothesis 6 of the Major Hypothesis 5

There will be no significant difference between the attitude of distance learners of various communities towards Evaluation: Assignments/Examinations conducted by IGNOU.

TABLE 4.45

Analysis Related to Community and Attitudes Towards Evaluation: Assignments and Examinations

Source	*D.F.*	*S.S.*	*M.S.S.*	*Fc*	*Ft*
Between groups	4	157.7	39.4	3.98*	2.37
Error	440	4288.9	70.7		
Total	**444**	**4546.6**			

* Significant at 0.05 per cent level.

From the Table 4.45 it could be seen that the F value is significant at 0.05 per cent level and therefore the null hypothesis is rejected; i.e. there is significant difference in the attitude of the learners belonging to the five community groups towards Evaluation: Assignments/Examinations conducted by IGNOU.

The statistical value related to the attitude is the highest for the learners belonging to Forward community followed by the Backward, Most Backward, Scheduled caste, and Scheduled tribes communities.

The attitudes of distance learners of various marital status towards the six aspects of IGNOU programmes were compared. The Table 4.46 provides the mean and standard deviation values of attitude of the learners towards various programmes and the same were compared using ANOVA. The ANOVA tables are as follows.

TABLE 4.46

Attitude of Distance Learners of Different Categories of Programmes Towards the Six Aspects of IGNOU Programmes

Six aspects of IGNOU program	*Married*		*Unmarried*		*Others*	
	Mean	*S.D.*	*Mean*	*S.D.*	*Mean*	*S.D.*
Admission Procedures	35.2	3.1	36.6	3.3	34.8	3.2
Self-Instructional Materials	38.1	2.6	39.3	2.4	37.9	2.4
Media-Television	36.3	2.7	35.2	2.6	34.8	2.8
Study Centre/ Library	34.4	2.8	35.6	2.7	33.8	2.6
Counsellors/ Counselling	41.9	2.8	43.2	2.9	41.7	2.8
Evaluation	43.3	2.9	43.5	3.0	43.2	3.1
Overall	**229.2**	**8.2**	**233.4**	**8.1**	**226.2**	**8.2**

Major Hypothesis 6

There will be is no significant difference between the attitude of the distance learners of various marital status towards six aspects of IGNOU programmes.

TABLE 4.47

Analysis Related to the Marital Status and the Six Aspects of IGNOU Programmes

Source	*D.F.*	*S.S.*	*M.S.S.*	*Fc*	*Ft*
Between groups	2	462.4	231.2	3.23*	2.99
Error	442	31616.6	71.5		
Total	444	32079.0			

* Significant at 0.05 per cent level.

From the Table 4.47 it is seen that the F value is significant at 0.05 per cent level and therefore the null hypothesis is rejected; i.e. there is significant difference in the attitude of the learners belonging to the three marital status groups towards the six aspects of IGNOU programmes.

The statistical value related to the attitude is the highest for learners belonging to unmarried learners followed by the married and others.

Sub-Hypothesis 1 of the Major Hypothesis 6

There will be no significant difference between attitude of distance learners of different marital status groups towards Admission procedures of IGNOU.

TABLE 4.48

Analysis of Attitude of Distance Learners to Marital Status and Admission Procedures

Source	*D.F.*	*S.S.*	*M.S.S.*	*Fc*	*Ft*
Between groups	2	95.9	47.9	1.90	2.99
Error	442	5036.7	11.3		
Total	**444**	**5132.6**			

From the Table 4.48 it could be seen that the F value is not significant at 0.05 per cent level and therefore the null hypothesis is rejected; i.e. there is no significant difference in the attitude of the learners belonging to the three marital status groups and towards admission procedures of IGNOU.

Sub-Hypothesis 2 of the Major Hypothesis 6

There will be no significant difference between the attitudes of distance learners of different marital status towards Self- Instruction Materials provided by IGNOU.

Table 4.49 it is observed the F value is significant at 0.05 per cent level and therefore the null hypothesis is rejected i.e., there is significant difference among the learners belonging to three marital status groups in the attitude towards Self-Instruction Material provided by IGNOU.

TABLE 4.49

Analysis Related to the Marital Status and the Attitude Towards Printed Self-Instruction Materials

Source	*D.F.*	*S.S.*	*M.S.S.*	*Fc*	*Ft*
Between groups	2	62.7	31.3	4.5*	2.99
Error	442	3174.1	7.2		
Total	**444**	**3236.8**			

* Significant at 0.05 per cent level.

The statistical value related to the attitude is the highest for the learners belonging to unmarried learners followed by the married and others.

Sub-Hypothesis 3 of the Major Hypothesis 6

There will be no significant difference between the attitude of distance learners of different marital status towards non-print material-Television programmes provided by IGNOU

TABLE 4.50

Analysis Related to the Marital Status and the Attitude Towards Non-Print Study Materials

Source	*D.F.*	*S.S.*	*M.S.S.*	*Fc*	*Ft*
Between groups	2	53.8	26.9	3.2*	2.99
Error	442	3680.2	8.3		
Total	444	3734.0			

* Significant at 0.05 per cent level.

From the Table 4.50 it could be seen that the F value is significant at 0.05 per cent level and therefore the null hypothesis is rejected; i.e. there is significant difference in the attitude of the learners belonging to the three marital status groups towards non-print materials - Television programmes provided by IGNOU.

The statistical value related to the attitude is the highest for the learners belonging to married learners followed by the unmarried and others.

Sub-Hypothesis 4 of the Major Hypothesis 6

There will be no significant difference between the attitude of distance learners of different marital status towards the study centres and library facilities provided by IGNOU.

TABLE 4.51

Analysis Related to the Marital Status and the Attitude Towards Study Centres/Library Facilities

Source	*D.F.*	*S.S.*	*M.S.S.*	*Fc*	*Ft*
Between groups	2	62.8	30.7	3.7*	2.99
Error	442	3671.8	8.3		
Total	**444**	**3734.0**			

*Significant at 0.05 per cent level.

From the Table 4.51 it could be seen that the F value is significant at 0.05 per cent level and therefore the null hypothesis is rejected; i.e. there is significant difference in the attitude of the learners belonging to the three marital status groups towards study centers/library facilities provided by IGNOU.

The statistical value related to the attitude is the highest for the learners belonging to unmarried learners followed by the married and others.

Sub-Hypothesis 5 of the Major Hypothesis 6

There will be no significant difference between the attitude of distance learners of different marital status towards the Counsellors/Counselling conducted by IGNOU.

TABLE 4.52

Analysis Related to the Marital Status and the Attitudes Towards Counsellers/Counselling

Source	*D.F.*	*S.S.*	*M.S.S.*	*Fc*	*Ft*
Between groups	2	70.2	35.1	3.7*	2.99
Error	442	4196.6	9.5		
Total	**444**	**4266.8**			

* Significant at 0.05 per cent level.

From the Table 4.52 it could be seen that the F value is significant at 0.05 per cent level and therefore the null hypothesis is rejected; i.e. there is significant difference in the attitude of the learners belonging to the three marital status groups towards the Counsellors/Counselling conducted by IGNOU.

The statistical value related to the attitude is the highest for the learners belonging to unmarried learners followed by the married and others.

Sub-Hypothesis 6 of the Major Hypothesis 6

There will be no significant difference between the attitude of distance learners of different marital status towards Evaluation: Assignments/Examinations conducted by IGNOU.

TABLE 4.53

Analysis Related to the Marital Status and the Attitude Towards Evaluation: Assignments and Examinations

Source	*D.F.*	*S.S.*	*M.S.S.*	*Fc*	*Ft*
Between groups	2	38.0	19.4	1.90	2.99
Error	442	4507.7	10.2		
Total	444	4546.6			

From the Table 4.53 it could be seen that the F value is no significant at 0.05 per cent level and therefore the null hypothesis is accepted; i.e. there is no significant difference in the attitude of the learners belonging to the three marital status groups towards Evaluation: Assignments/Examinations conducted by IGNOU.

TABLE 4.54

Attitude of Distance Learners with Various Educational Background Towards the Six Aspects of IGNOU Programmes

Six aspects of IGNOU program	*Upto+2 level*		*Under. graduate*		*Post graduate*		*Professional*		*Technical*	
	Mean	*S.D.*	*Mean*	*S.D.*	*Mean*	*S.D.*	*Mean*	*S.D.*	*Mean*	*S.D.*
Admission Procedures	33.2	3.0	35.6	3.1	37.5	3.3	38.2	3.3	38.6	3.2
Self-Instructional Materials	35.3	2.3	36.6	2.8	37.3	3.1	38.4	2.5	39.6	2.6
Media-Television	33.2	2.5	33.8	3.1	34.6	2.5	36.6	2.6	37.1	2.8
Study Centre/Library	31.6	2.6	32.4	2.8	33.8	2.8	35.4	2.9	36.1	3.0
Counsellors/ Counselling	41.6	3.1	42.1	3.0	42.0	3.0	42.2	2.9	39.8	2.8
Evaluation	40.4	2.9	41.6	3.2	41.8	3.2	42.9	3.2	43.9	2.9
Overall	**215.3**	**7.6**	**222.1**	**8.2**	**227.0**	**8.5**	**233.7**	**8.1**	**235.1**	**8.9**

The attitudes of distance learners with different educational background towards the six aspects of IGNOU programmes were compared. The Table 4.54 provides the mean and standard deviation of educational background and it is compared using ANOVA. The ANOVA tables are furnished as follows:

Major Hypothesis 7

There will be no significant difference between the attitude of the distance learners of various educational background towards six aspects of IGNOU programmes.

TABLE 4.55

Analysis Related to the Educational Background and Six Aspects of IGNOU Programmes

Source	*D.F.*	*S.S.*	*M.S.S.*	*Fc*	*Ft*
Between groups	4	1454.2	363.6	5.22*	2.37
Error	440	30624.8	69.8		
Total	**444**	**32079.0**			

* Significant at 0.05 per cent level.

From the Table 4.55 it is seen that the F value is significant at 0.05 per cent level and therefore the null hypothesis is rejected; i.e. there is significant difference in the attitude of the learners belonging to the various educational background towards the six aspects of IGNOU programmes.

The statistical value related to the attitude is the highest for learners belonging to technical followed by the professional, Postgraduate, Undergraduate, and upto +2 level.

Sub-Hypothesis 1 of the Major Hypothesis 7

There will be no significant difference between attitude of distance learners of various educational background towards Admission procedures of IGNOU.

As per the Table 4.56 it could be seen that the F value is significant at 0.05 per cent level and therefore the null hypothesis is rejected; i.e. there is significant difference in the attitude of the learners belonging to various educational background towards admission procedures of IGNOU.

TABLE 4.56

Analysis Attitude of Distance Learners to Educational Background and Attitudes Towards Admission Procedures of IGNOU

Source	*D.F.*	*S.S.*	*M.S.S.*	*Fc*	*Ft*
Between groups	4	216.2	54.1	4.83*	2.37
Error	440	4916.4	11.2		
Total	444	5132.6			

*Significant at 0.05 per cent level.

The statistical value related to attitude is the highest for the learners belonging to technical followed by the Professional, Post-graduate, Undergraduate, and Upto +2 level.

Sub-Hypothesis 2 of the Major Hypothesis 7

There will be no significant difference between attitudes of distance learners of Various educational background towards Self- Instruction Materials provided by IGNOU.

TABLE 4.57

Analysis Related to Educational Background and Attitude Towards Printed Self- Instruction Materials

Source	*D.F.*	*S.S.*	*M.S.S.*	*Fc*	*Ft*
Between groups	4	98.2	24.5	3.45*	2.37
Error	440	3138.6	7.1		
Total	**444**	**3236.8**			

*Significant at 0.05 per cent level.

From the Table 4.57 it is observed the F value is significant at 0.05 per cent level and therefore the null hypothesis is rejected; i.e. there is significant difference of the learners belonging to various educational background in the attitude towards Self- Instruction Material provided by IGNOU.

The statistical value related to the attitude is the highest for the learners with Technical education followed by the Professional, Post-graduate, Undergraduate, and upto +2 level.

Sub-Hypothesis 3 of the Major Hypothesis 7

There will be no significant difference between the attitude of distance learners of various educational background towards non-print material-Television programmes provided by IGNOU.

TABLE 4.58

Analysis Related to the Educational Background and Attitude Towards Non-Print Study Materials

Source	*D.F.*	*S.S.*	*M.S.S.*	*Fc*	*Ft*
Between groups	4	152.2	38.1	4.69*	2.37
Error	440	3581.8	8.1		
Total	**444**	**3734.0**			

* Significant at 0.05 per cent level.

From the Table 4.58 it could be seen that the F value is significant at 0.05 per cent level and therefore the null hypothesis is rejected; i.e. there is significant difference in the attitude of the learners belonging to various educational background towards non-print materials - Television programmes provided by IGNOU.

The statistical value related to attitude is the highest for the learners with Technical education followed by the Professional, Post-graduate, Undergraduate, and upto +2 level.

Sub-Hypothesis 4 of the Major Hypothesis 7

There will be no significant difference between the attitude of distance learners of various educational background towards study centres and library facilities provided by IGNOU.

TABLE 4.59

Analysis Related to the Educational Background and the Attitude Towards Study Centres/Library Facilities

Source	*D.F.*	*S.S.*	*M.S.S.*	*Fc*	*Ft*
Between groups	4	99.6	24.9	3.0*	2.37
Error	440	3634.4	8.3		
Total	**444**	**3734.0**			

*Significant at 0.05 per cent level.

From the Table 4.59 it could be seen that the F value is significant at 0.05 per cent level and therefore the null hypothesis is rejected; i.e. there is significant difference in the attitude of the learners belonging to educational background towards study centers/library facilities provided by IGNOU.

The statistical value related to the attitude is the highest for the learners with Technical education followed by the Professional, Post-graduate, Undergraduate, and upto +2 level.

Sub-Hypothesis 5 of the Major Hypothesis 7

There will be no significant difference between the attitude of distance learners of various educational background towards Counsellors/Counselling conducted by IGNOU.

TABLE 4.60

Analysis Related to the Educational Background and the Attitudes Towards Counselors/Counselling

Source	*D.F.*	*S.S.*	*M.S.S.*	*Fc*	*Ft*
Between groups	4	52.6	13.1	1.4	2.37
Error	440	4214.2	9.5		
Total	**444**	**4266.8**			

From the Table 4.60 it could be seen that the F value is no

significant at 0.05 per cent level and therefore the null hypothesis is accepted; i.e. there is no significant difference in the attitude of the learners belonging to various educational background towards Counsellors/Counselling conducted by IGNOU.

Sub-Hypothesis 6 of the Major Hypothesis 7

There will be no significant difference between the attitude of distance learners of various educational background towards Evaluation: Assignments/Examinations conducted by IGNOU

TABLE 4.61

Analysis Related to the Educational Background and the Attitudes Towards Evaluation: Assignments and Examinations

Source	*D.F.*	*S.S.*	*M.S.S.*	*Fc*	*Ft*
Between groups	4	139.4	34.8	3.5*	2.37
Error	440	4407.2	10.0		
Total	**444**	**4546.6**			

*Significant at 0/05 per cent level.

From the Table 4.61 it could be seen that the F value is significant at 0.05 per cent level and therefore the null hypothesis is rejected; i.e. there is significant difference in the attitude of the learners belonging to various educational background towards Evaluation: Assignments/Examinations conducted by IGNOU.

The statistical value related to the attitude is the highest for the learners belonging to Technical education followed by the Professional, Post-graduate, Undergraduate, and upto +2 level.The attitude of the distance learners belonging to various occupational status towards the six aspects of IGNOU programmes were compared. The Table 4.62 provides the mean and standard deviation of various occupational status and were compared using ANOVA. The ANOVA tables are as follows:

TABLE 4.62

Attitude of the Distance Learners with Various Occupational Status Towards the Six Aspects of IGNOU Programmes

Six aspects of IGNOU program	*Employed*		*Unemployed*		*Business*		*Traditional*		*Housewife*	
	Mean	*S.D.*	*Mean*	*S.D.*	*Mean*	*S.D.*	*Mean*	*S.D.*	*Mean*	*S.D.*
Admission Procedures	35.3	3.2	35.1	3.0	35.6	3.1	35.5	3.2	35.1	3.0
Self-Instructional Materials	37.8	2.6	38.0	2.7	38.3	2.7	38.1	2.9	38.2	2.8
Media-Television	34.8	2.7	35.0	2.8	34.9	3.0	35.2	2.9	35.1	3.1
Study Centre/Library	33.8	2.8	34.3	2.6	34.1	2.8	34.0	2.9	33.9	3.1
Counsellors/ Counselling	42.3	3.0	42.0	3.1	41.9	3.2	42.4	2.8	42.2	2.9
Evaluation	43.4	3.1	43.6	3.0	42.8	3.1	42.7	2.9	43.5	3.0
Overall	**227.4**	**7.9**	**228.0**	**8.4**	**227.6**	**8.2**	**227.9**	**8.3**	**228.0**	**8.4**

Major Hypothesis 8

There will be no significant difference between the attitude of the distance learners of various occupational status towards six aspects of IGNOU programmes.

TABLE 4.63

Analysis Related to Various Occupational Status and Six Aspects of IGNOU Programmes

Source	*D.F.*	*S.S.*	*M.S.S.*	*Fc*	*Ft*
Between groups	4	284.4	71.1	0.98*	N.S.
Error	440	31794.6	72.3		
Total	**444**	**32079.0**			

From the Table 4.63 it is seen that the F value is not significant at 0.05 per cent level and therefore the null hypothesis is accepted; i.e. there is no significant difference in the attitude of the learners belonging to various occupational groups towards the six aspects of IGNOU programmes.

Sub-Hypothesis 1 of the Major Hypothesis 8

There will be no significant difference between the attitude of distance learners of various occupational status towards the admission procedures of IGNOU.

TABLE 4.64

Analysis of the Attitude of Distance Learners to Various Occupational Status Towards Admission Procedures

Source	*D.F.*	*S.S.*	*M.S.S.*	*Fc*	*Ft*
Between groups	4	52.8	13.2	1.1	2.37
Error	440	5079.8	11.5		
Total	**444**	**5132.6**			

From the Table 4.64 it could be seen that the F value is no significant at 0.05 per cent level and therefore the null hypothesis is accepted; i.e. there is no significant difference in the attitude of the learners belonging to various occupational status towards admission procedures of IGNOU.

Sub-Hypothesis 2 of the Major Hypothesis 8

There will be no significant difference between the attitudes of distance learners of different occupational status towards Self- Instruction Materials provided by IGNOU.

From the Table 4.65 it is observed the F value, is not significant at 0.05 per cent level and therefore the null hypothesis is accepted; i.e. there is no significant difference in the attitude of the learners belonging to various occupational status towards Self- Instruction Material provided by IGNOU.

TABLE 4.65

Analysis Related to Various Occupational Status and the Attitude Towards Printed Self- Instruction Materials

Source	*D.F.*	*S.S.*	*M.S.S.*	*Fc*	*Ft*
Between groups	4	34.6	8.6	1.2	2.37
Error	440	3202.2	7.3		
Total	**444**	**3236.8**			

Sub-Hypothesis 3 of the Major Hypothesis 8

There will be no significant difference between attitude of distance learners of various occupational status towards non-print media -Television programmes provided by IGNOU.

TABLE 4.66

Analysis Related to Various Occupational Status and the Attitude Towards Non-Print Study Materials

Source	*D.F.*	*S.S.*	*M.S.S.*	*Fc*	*Ft*
Between groups	4	36.8	9.2	1.1	2.37
Error	440	3697.2	8.4		
Total	**444**	**3734.0**			

From the Table 4.66 it could be seen that the F value is not significant at 0.05 per cent level and therefore the null hypothesis is accepted; i.e. there is no significant difference in the attitude of the learners belonging to various educational background towards non-print media - Television programmes provided by IGNOU.

Sub-Hypothesis 4 of the Major Hypothesis 8

There will be no significant difference between attitude

of distance learners of various occupational status towards study centres and library facilities provided by IGNOU.

TABLE 4.67

Analysis Related to Various Occupational Status and Their Attitude Towards Study Centres/Library Facilities

Source	*D.F.*	*S.S.*	*M.S.S.*	*Fc*	*Ft*
Between groups	4	35.6	8.9	1.05	2.37
Error	440	3698.0	8.4		
Total	**444**	**3733.6**			

* Significant at 0.05 per cent level.

From the Table 4.67 it could be seen that the F value is no significant at 0.05 per cent level and therefore the null hypothesis is accepted; i.e. there is no significant difference in the attitude of the learners belonging to various occupational status towards study centers/library facilities provided by IGNOU.

Sub-Hypothesis 5 of the Major Hypothesis 8

There will be no significant difference between the attitude of distance learners of various occupational status towards Counsellors/Counselling conducted by IGNOU.

TABLE 4.68

Analysis Related to Various Occupational Status and the Attitudes Towards Counsellers/Counselling

Source	*D.F.*	*S.S.*	*M.S.S.*	*Fc*	*Ft*
Between groups	4	40.4	101.1	1.1	2.37
Error	440	4226.6	9.6		
Total	**444**	**4266.8**			

From the Table 4.68 it could be seen that the F value is no significant at 0.05 per cent level and therefore the null hypothesis is accepted; i.e. there is no significant difference in the attitude of the learners belonging to various occupational status towards Counsellors/Counselling conducted by IGNOU.

Sub-Hypothesis 6 of the Major Hypothesis 8

There will be no significant difference between the attitude of distance learners of various occupational status towards Evaluation: Assignments/Examinations conducted by IGNOU.

TABLE 4.69

Analysis Related Various Occupational Status and the Attitude Towards Evaluation: Assignments and Examinations

Source	*D.F.*	*S.S.*	*M.S.S.*	*Fc*	*Ft*
Between groups	4	53.4	13.4	1.31	2.37
Error	440	4493.2	10.2		
Total	**444**	**4546.6**			

TABLE 4.70

Attitude of the Distance Learners with the Various Income Groups Towards the Six Aspects of IGNOU Programmes

Six aspects of	*Upto 2000*		*2001-2004*		*4001-6000*		*6001-8000*		*8001 & above*	
IGNOU program	*Mean*	*S.D.*	*Mean*	*S.D.*	*Mean*	*S.D.*	*Mean*	*S.D.*	*Mean*	*S.D.*
Admission Procedures	37.4	3.0	37.9	2.8	36.3	2.9	34.6	2.4	34.1	2.6
Self-Instructional Materials	37.8	2.2	37.6	2.1	38.1	2.3	38.3	2.1	39.4	2.2
Media-Television	34.6	2.3	34.5	2.2	35.0	2.6	35.4	2.1	35.6	2.2
Study Centre/Library	35.1	2.1	35.3	2.3	34.3	2.1	33.8	2.1	33.3	2.3
Counsellors/ Counselling	43.5	2.6	43.3	2.5	42.2	2.7	41.8	2.4	41.6	2.5
Evaluation	43.7	2.6	43.5	2.7	43.4	2.5	43.2	2.4	43.1	2.2
Overall	**231.1**	**8.1**	**232.1**	**8.4**	**229.3**	**7.9**	**227.1**	**8.0**	**226.1**	**8.1**

From the Table 4.69 it could be seen that the F value is not significant at 0.05 per cent level and therefore the null hypothesis is accepted; i.e. there is no significant difference in the attitude of the learners belonging to various occupational status towards Evaluation: Assignments/Examinations conducted by IGNOU.

The attitudes of distance learners at different income groups towards the six aspects of IGNOU programmes were compared. The Table 4.70 provides the mean and standard deviation of five income groups and were compared using ANOVA. The ANOVA tables are as follows:

Major Hypothesis 9

There will be no significant difference between the attitude of the distance learners of different income groups towards six aspects of IGNOU programmes.

TABLE 4.71

Analysis Related to the Various Income Groups and Six Aspects of IGNOU Programmes

Source	*D.F.*	*S.S.*	*M.S.S.*	*Fc*	*Ft*
Between groups	4	1886.3	471.6	6.87*	2.21
Error	440	30192.7	68.6		
Total	**444**	**32079.0**			

* Significant at 0.05 per cent level.

From the Table 4.71 it is seen that the F value is significant at 0.05 per cent level and therefore the null hypothesis is rejected; i.e. there is significant difference in the attitude of the learners belonging to five income groups towards the six aspects of IGNOU programmes.

The statistical value related to the attitude is the highest for learners belonging to the income group of Rs. 8001 and above followed by income group of 6001-8000, 4001-6000, Upto Rs. 2000 and 2001-4000.

Sub-Hypothesis 1 of the Major Hypothesis 9

There will be no significant difference between the attitude of distance learners of different family income groups towards the Admission procedures of IGNOU.

TABLE 4.72

Analysis of the Attitude of Distance Learners of the Various Income Groups and Their Attitudes Towards Admission Procedures

Source	*D.F.*	*S.S.*	*M.S.S.*	*Fc*	*Ft*
Between groups	4	272.6	68.2	6.2*	2.21
Error	440	4860.0	11.0		
Total	**444**	**5132.6**			

* Significant at 0.05 per cent level.

From the Table 4.72 it could be seen that the F value is significant at 0.05 per cent level and therefore the null hypothesis is rejected; i.e. there is significant difference in the attitude of the learners belonging to five income groups towards admission procedures of IGNOU

The statistical value related to the attitude is the highest for the learners belonging to the income group of Rs. 2001-4000 followed by income groups of Upto. Rs. 2000, 4001-6000, 6001-8000 and 8001 and above.

Sub-Hypothesis 2 of the Major Hypothesis 9

There will be no significant difference between attitudes of distance learners of different income groups towards Self-Instruction Materials provided by IGNOU.

TABLE 4.73

Analysis Related to the Various Income Groups and Their Attitude Towards Printed Self- Instruction Materials

Source	*D.F.*	*S.S.*	*M.S.S.*	*Fc*	*Ft*
Between groups	4	155.6	38.9	5.55*	2.21
Error	440	3081.2	7.0		
Total	**444**	**3234.8**			

*Significant at 0.05 per cent level.

From the Table 4.73 it is observed that the F value is significant at 0.05 per cent level and therefore the null hypothesis is rejected; i.e. there is significant difference in the attitude of the learners belonging to five income groups towards Self- Instruction Material provided by IGNOU.

The statistical value related to the attitude is the highest for the learners belonging to the income group of Rs.8001 and above followed by income group of Rs. 6001-8000, 4001-6000, Upto Rs. 2000 and 2001-4000.

Sub-Hypothesis 3 of the Major Hypothesis 9

There will be no significant difference between attitude of distance learners of different income groups towards non-print material-Television programmes provided by IGNOU.

TABLE 4.74

Analysis Related to the Various Income Groups and Their Attitude Towards Non-Print Study Materials

Source	*D.F.*	*S.S.*	*M.S.S.*	*Fc*	*Ft*
Between groups	4	188.3	47.1	5.81*	2.21
Error	440	3545.7	8.1		
Total	**444**	**3734.0**			

*Significant at 0.05 per cent level.

From the Table 4.74 it could be seen that the F value is significant at 0.05 per cent level and therefore the null hypothesis is rejected; i.e. there is significant difference in the attitude of the learners belonging to five income groups towards Non-Print Materials -Television programmes provided by IGNOU.

The statistical value related to attitude is the highest for the learners belonging to the income group of Rs.8001 and above followed by income group of Rs.6001-8000, 4001-6000, Upto Rs.2000 and 2001-4000.

Sub-Hypothesis 4 of the Major Hypothesis 9

There will be no significant difference between attitude of distance learners of different income groups towards study centres and library facilities provided by IGNOU.

TABLE 4.75

Analysis Related to the Various Income Groups and Their Attitude Towards Study Centres/Library Facilities

Source	*D.F.*	*S.S.*	*M.S.S.*	*Fc*	*Ft*
Between groups	4	176.2	44.1	5.4*	2.21
Error	440	3557.8	8.1		
Total	**444**	**3734.0**			

* Significant at 0.05 per cent level.

From the Table 4.75 it could be seen that the F value is significant at 0.05 per cent level and therefore the null hypothesis is rejected; i.e. there is significant difference in the attitude of the learners belonging to five income groups towards study centers/library facilities provided by IGNOU.

The statistical value related to the attitude is the highest for the learners belonging to the income group of Rs. 2001-4000 followed by income group of Upto Rs. 2000, 4001-6000, 6001-8000, and 8001 and above.

Sub-Hypothesis 5 of the Major Hypothesis 9

There will be no significant difference between the attitude of distance learners of the different income groups towards Counsellors/Counselling conducted by IGNOU.

TABLE 4.76

Analysis Related to the Various Income Groups and Their Attitudes Towards Counselors/Counselling

Source	*D.F.*	*S.S.*	*M.S.S.*	*Fc*	*Ft*
Between groups	4	208.6	52.2	5.7*	2.21
Error	440	4058.2	9.2		
Total	**444**	**4266.8**			

From the Table 4.76 it could be seen that the F value is significant at 0.05 per cent level and therefore the null hypothesis is accepted; i.e. there is significant difference in the attitude of the learners belonging to five income groups towards Counsellors/Counselling conducted by IGNOU.

The statistical value related to attitude is the highest for the learners belonging to the income group of Rs. Upto Rs.2000 followed by the income group of Rs.2001-4000, 4001-6000, 6001-8000, and 8001 and above.

Sub-Hypothesis 6 of the Major Hypothesis 9

There will be no significant difference between the attitude of distance learners of different family income groups towards Evaluation: Assignments/Examinations conducted by IGNOU.

From the Table 4.77 it could be seen that the F value is significant at 0.05 per cent level and therefore the null hypothesis is rejected; i.e. there is significant difference in the attitude of the learners belonging to five income groups towards Evaluation: Assignments/Examinations conducted by IGNOU.

TABLE 4.77

Analysis Related to the Various Income Groups and Their Attitudes Towards Evaluation: Assignments and Examinations

Source	*D.F.*	*S.S.*	*M.S.S.*	*Fc*	*Ft*
Between groups	4	165.4	41.4	4.2*	2.21
Error	440	4381.2	9.95		
Total	**444**	**4546.6**			

*Significant at 0.05 per cent level.

The statistical value related to attitude is the highest for the learners belonging to the income group of Upto Rs.2000 followed by income group of Rs.2001-4000, 4001-6000, 6001-8000, and 8001 and above.

PART - II

In this part, the analysis deals with the attitude of the distance learners based on sex, residence and type of family variables and the *'t'* tests were employed to test the hypotheses.

Hypothesis

There will be no significant difference in attitude between the male and female distance learners towards six aspects of IGNOU programmes.

As per the *'t'* test results there is a significant (0.05 per cent level) relationship between attitudes of male and female and six aspects of IGNOU programmes. The evaluation dimension has not emerged significantly out of the listed variables.

Hypothesis

There will be no significant difference in attitude between the rural and urban distance learners towards six aspects of IGNOU programmes.

TABLE 4.78

Attitude of Distance Learners in Male and Female Towards the Six Aspects of IGNOU Programmes

Six aspects of IGNOU program	*MALE*		*FEMALE*		*'T' Level of Significance (%)*	
	Mean	*S.D.*	*Mean*	*S.D.*	*Mean*	*S.D.*
Admission Procedures	36.2	3.1	33.9	3.0	5.79	0.05
Self-Instructional Materials	37.8	3.1	39.8	3.1	4.81	0.05
Media-Television	34.4	3.0	38.2	3.2	9.3	0.05
Study Centre/ Library	33.5	2.7	37.1	2.6	9.98	0.05
Counsellors/ Counselling	41.3	3.0	44.2	2.8	7.71	0.05
Evaluation	43.1	3.0	43.6	2.9	1.23	N.S.
Overall	**226.4**	**8.1**	**236.8**	**7.2**	**9.33**	**0.05**

TABLE 4.79

Attitude of the Distance Learners in Rural and Urban Areas Towards the Six Aspects of IGNOU Programmes

Six aspects of IGNOU program	*RURAL*		*URBAN*		*'T' Level of Significance (%)*	
	Mean	*S.D.*	*Mean*	*S.D.*	*Mean*	*S.D.*
Admission Procedures	34.6	3.3	36.7	3.2	6.81	0.05
Self-Instructional Materials	37.1	2.6	39.6	2.7	9.9	0.05
Media-Television	33.5	2.9	38.2	2.8	17.4	0.05
Study Centre/ Library	32.9	2.8	36.1	2.7	12.3	0.05
Counsellors/ Counselling	40.6	3.1	45.0	3.0	8.3	0.05
Evaluation	43.2	3.1	43.5	3.0	1.03	N.S.
Overall	**221.9**	**8.3**	**239.1**	**8.0**	**19.6**	**0.05**

As per the '*t*' test results there is a significant (0.05 percent level) relationship between attitudes of the learners of rural and urban and six aspects of IGNOU programmes. The evaluation dimension has not emerged significantly out of the listed variables.

Hypothesis

There will be no significant difference in attitude between the nuclear and joint family distance learners towards six aspects of IGNOU programmes.

TABLE 4.80

Attitude of Distance Learners in the Nuclear and Joint Family Towards the Six Aspects of IGNOU Programmes

Six aspects of IGNOU program	*Nuclear Family*		*Joint Family*		*'T' Level of Significance (%)*	
	Mean	*S.D.*	*Mean*	*S.D.*	*Mean*	*S.D.*
Admission Procedures	35.1	3.2	36.3	3.1	4.01	0.05
Self-Instructional Materials	39.8	2.4	37.2	2.6	10.9	0.05
Media-Television	34.0	2.7	36.2	2.8	8.4	0.05
Study Centre/ Library	33.8	3.0	35.2	2.9	4.9	0.05
Counsellors/ Counselling	43.1	2.9	41.6	2.8	5.5	0.05
Evaluation	43.3	3.0	43.5	2.9	0.71	N.S
Overall	**229.1**	**8.1**	**230.0**	**8.3**	**1.2**	**N.S**

As per the '*t*' test results there is a significant (0.05 percent level) relationship between attitudes of Nuclear and Joint family learners and six aspects of IGNOU programmes. The evaluation dimension has not emerged significantly out of the listed variables.

PART-III

In this part, the analysis deals with the relationship between education, occupation and attitude of distance learners towards the six aspects of IGNOU programmes. The correlation technique is employed to find out the relationship.

Hypothesis

There will be no significant relationship between the parent's education, occupation and the attitude of distance learners towards six aspects of IGNOU programmes.

TABLE 4.81

Correlation Between Parents Education, Occupation and the Attitude of the Distance Learners Towards Six Aspects of IGNOU Programmes

Six aspects of IGNOU program	*Education*	*'T' Level of Significance (%)*	*Occupation*	*'T' Level of Significance (%)*
Admission Procedures	0.49	0.05	0.32	0.05
Self-Instructional Materials	0.58	0.05	0.38	0.05
Media-Television	0.54	0.05	0.41	0.05
Study Centre/ Library	0.62	0.05	0.37	0.05
Counsellors/ Counselling	0.65	0.05	0.36	0.05
Evaluation	0.48	0.05	0.28	0.05
Overall	**0.61**	**0.05**	**0.35**	**0.05**

All the correlations are found to be significant at 0.05 per cent level and correlations are also positive and that the

Parent's education and occupation are related to attitude of distance learners towards six aspects of IGNOU programmes.

Summary

In this chapter, the data collected were analyzed and the results were interpreted. The first part of the chapter, dealt with the various study centres, programmes, age, religion, community, marital status and income of distance learners and their attitude towards six aspect of IGNOU programmes. The second part of the analysis dealt with the attitude of the distance learners based on variables such as sex, residence and type of family. The third part of the analysis dealt with the relationship between parent's education, occupation and attitude of distance learners towards the six aspects of IGNOU programmes.

In the following chapter the summary of the findings, conclusion and suggestions for further study are presented.

5

Findings and Conclusion

The data collected for the investigation have been analyzed and the findings are presented in this chapter. A brief summary of the investigation, the findings, discussion and conclusions that have been drawn from the statistical analysis are discussed.

Findings of the Study

PART-I

The major findings of the present study are:

There is significant difference in the attitude of distance learners belonging to different study centres towards

1. Admission Procedures
2. Printed Self-Instructional Materials
3. Non-Print Material - IGNOU Television Programmes
4. Study Centre/Library Facilities
5. Counsellors/Counselling Services
6. Evaluation: Assignment/Examinations.

There is significant difference in the attitude of distance learners belonging to different programmes towards

1. Admission Procedures
2. Printed Self-Instructional Materials

3. Non-Print Material - IGNOU Television Programmes
4. Evaluation: Assignment/Examinations

There is no significant difference in the attitude of distance learners belonging to different programmes towards

1. Study Centre/Library Facilities
2. Counsellors/Counselling Services.

There is significant difference in the attitude of distance learners belonging to various age groups towards

1. Admission Procedures
2. Printed Self-Instructional Materials
3. Non-Print Material - IGNOU Television Programmes
4. Study Centre/Library Facilities
5. Counsellors/Counselling Services
6. Evaluation: Assignment/Examinations.

There is significant difference in the attitude of distance learners belonging to different religions towards

1. Admission Procedures
2. Printed Self-Instructional Materials
3. Non-Print Material - IGNOU Television Programmes
4. Study Centre/Library Facilities
5. Counsellors/Counselling Services
6. Evaluation: Assignment/Examinations.

There is significant difference in the attitude of distance learners belonging to various communities towards

1. Admission Procedures
2. Printed Self-Instructional Materials
3. Non-Print Material - IGNOU Television Programmes

4. Study Centre/Library Facilities
5. Counsellors/Counselling Services
6. Evaluation: Assignment/Examinations.

There is significant difference in the attitude of distance learners belonging to various marital status towards

1. Printed Self-Instructional Materials
2. Non-Print Material - IGNOU Television Programmes
3. Study Centre/Library Facilities
4. Counsellors/Counselling Services.

There is no significant difference in the attitude of distance learners belonging to various marital status towards

1. Admission Procedures
2. Evaluation: Assignment/Examinations.

There is significant difference in the attitude of distance learners belonging to various educational backgrounds towards

1. Admission Procedures
2. Printed Self-Instructional Materials
3. Non-Print Material - IGNOU Television Programmes
4. Study Centre/Library Facilities
5. Evaluation: Assignment/Examinations.

There is significant difference in the attitude of distance learners belonging to various educational background towards

1. Counsellors/Counselling Services.

There is no significant difference in the attitude of distance learners belonging to various occupational status towards

1. Admission Procedures
2. Printed Self-Instructional Materials

3. Non-Print Material - IGNOU Television Programmes
4. Study Centre/Library Facilities
5. Counsellors/Counselling Services
6. Evaluation: Assignment/Examinations.

There is significant difference in the attitude of distance learners belonging to various income groups towards

1. Admission Procedures
2. Printed Self-Instructional Materials
3. Non-Print Material - IGNOU Television Programmes
4. Study Centre/Library Facilities
5. Counsellors/Counselling Services
6. Evaluation: Assignment/Examinations.

PART - II

There is significant difference in the attitude of distance learners belonging to different sex towards

1. Admission Procedures
2. Printed Self-Instructional Materials
3. Non-Print Material - IGNOU Television Programmes
4. Study Centre/Library Facilities
5. Counsellors/Counselling Services.

There is no significant difference in the attitude of distance learners belonging to different sex towards

1. Evaluation: Assignment/Examinations.

There is significant difference in the attitude of distance learners belonging to different localities towards

1. Admission Procedures
2. Printed Self-Instructional Materials
3. Non-Print Material - IGNOU Television Programmes

4. Study Centre/Library Facilities
5. Counsellors/Counselling Services.

There is no significant difference in the attitude of distance learners belonging to different localities towards

1. Evaluation: Assignment/Examinations.

There is significant difference in the attitude of distance learners belonging to different types of families towards

1. Admission Procedures
2. Printed Self-Instructional Materials
3. Non-Print Material - IGNOU Television Programmes
4. Study Centre/Library Facilities
5. Counsellors/Counselling Services.

There is no significant difference in the attitude of distance learners belonging to different types of families towards

1. Evaluation: Assignment/Examinations

There is significant difference in the attitude of distance learners having parents with different educational background towards

1. Admission Procedures
2. Printed Self-Instructional Materials
3. Non-Print Material - IGNOU Television Programmes
4. Study Centre/Library Facilities
5. Counsellors/Counselling Services
6. Evaluation: Assignment/Examinations.

PART-III

There is significant difference in the attitude of distance learners parents with different occupational status towards

1. Admission Procedures

2. Printed Self-Instructional Materials
3. Non-Print Material—IGNOU Television Programmes
4. Study Centre/Library Facilities
5. Counsellors/Counselling Services
6. Evaluation: Assignment/Examinations.

Conclusion

The investigation is in the attitude of distance learners towards Admission Procedures of the IGNOU, Printed Self-Instructional Materials, Non-Print Material-IGNOU Television Programmes, Study Centre/Library Facilities, Counsellors/Counselling Services and Evaluation comprising assignment and examinations. The choice of location for purposes of selection of subjects are centred around Madras, Coimbatore, Tiruchirapalli and Madurai.

An indepth analysis of the study reveals certain interesting features, which can be considered by policy makers of open university system in India to provide an effective open learning environment. In all social development activities the aim is to apprehend, analyse, reinforce or modify the attitude of learners by implementing development activities tuned to the needs of the target group. In this process the attitude remains as the core variable, which is strengthened or modified depending upon the context. For this study, attitude has been chosen as an important variable and studied the attitudinal dispositions of the distance learners of IGNOU towards certain chosen aspects of the open university system, since it would provide feed back to the distance education administrators, so that necessary changes in the delivery system of distance education could be made to make distance education effective.

The attitude of learners enrolled in various distance education programmes of IGNOU centres located at Madras,

Coimbatore, Tiruchirapalli, and Madurai indicate certain dissimilarities in their attitude towards the six aspects of IGNOU's delivery system including admission procedures. The value dimension of the attitude is favourable in respect of learners attached to Chennai study center. The value dimension is also favourable in respect of learners and there is no significant difference among the learners belonging to different religions and occupational groups.

The study among other things focuses on the aspect of distance education, viz., self-instructional material. The findings confirms that distance learners attitude towards self-instructional material is significant. Therefore, the distance education administrators should take serious note of this and plan for good quality printed materials in attractive format and its supply within the time frame. In a populated country like India an average learner aspires to enroll in a meaningful credential programme which is linked to fair and objective, admission enrollment procedure.

The result reveals that learners in the Chennai study center have a favourable attitude towards IGNOU programmes than the learners at the other five study centres. Learners at the other study centres pointed out that some of them did not receive self-instructional material in time. Also they do not make use of the study center library facilities to the optimum level. Receipt of counselling session also seems to be irregular at the Chennai study center. By the same token it is construed that only metropolition study centres, receive attention than the other study centres.

From the response of the learners it is observed that the post-graduate learners are the most satisfied with self-instructional materials. The analysis also indicates that the IGNOU programmes are more attractive to the age group of 16-25 than to the other age groups. The results indicate the remarkable diversity of clientele system and their attitude towards certain chosen variables.

The findings of this research may be used for conducting open learning systems successfully. Evaluation and feedback must be obtained from the beneficiaries for policy analysis and for implementation of strategic plans.

Suggestion for Future Research

1. Recommend similar study at different states of India and other Asian countries where open university system are prevalent.
2. Suggest similar research relating to study centres utilizing the counselling and library facilities by distance learners.
3. Recommend research relating to cost benefit analysis of open university system.
4. Suggest similar research to utilize multimedia for facilitating learning by distance learners.
5. Recommend similar research related to diagnosing dropouts and familiarity counseling procedures.
6. Recommend similar research related to printed self-instructional materials utilized by autonomous learners for assessing its efficacy.

Bibliography

Adiseshiah, M.S. (1990), "Strategies for Distance Education", *Kakatiya Journal of Distance Education*, School of Distance Learning and Continuing Education, Kakatiya University, A.P., July- December, Vol.1, No.2.

Ahmad Shakeel (2004), "Significance of Distance Education in India", *University News*, Vol. 42, No. 34, August 23-29.

Alan Tait (ed.) (1993), *Key Issues in Open Learning*, Longman, London.

Ananthasayanam, R. et al. (1988), "Role of Television in Distance Education: An Experience from Education Television (ETV) Programme of Madras Doordharsan", *Journal of Educational Planning and Administration*, Vol.2, No.3 & 4, Special edition on Distance Education, Ed. M. Mukopadhyay, New Delhi.

Anderson, H.T. et al. (1977), "An exploratory study of Correspondence Courses", Unpublished manuscript, University of Illinois, Champaign Verbara, ERIC Document Reproduction, No.Ed 013371.

Antonia M. Alvarez (1990), "Research into Post Graduate Distance Education", Education of the course on translation studies at UNED, Spain.

Anil Yadav (1993), "Open Learning System: A model for conceptual analysis", *Indian Journal of Open Learning*, Vol. 2, No.2, IGNOU, New Delhi.

Arora Asha (1994), "Distance Education", *University News*, Vol. XXXII, No.21, May 23.

Baath J.A. (1980), *Postal Two Way Communication in Correspondence Education*, Lund; Gleerup.

Bae Cheon (1984), "Comparative Study of the Open University of Britain the Air and Correspondence College of Korea", Michigan University.

Bahugune, R.C. (1986), "A Comprehensive Study of Correspondence and Formal Education", Ph.D. thesis, Meerut University.

Beyth Maron, et al. (1988), "Tutor and course coordinator hierarchical relationships and Mutual Perceptions in Developing Distance Education", Ed. David Sewart and John Danial. Oslo, ICDE 14th World Conference Papers.

Bloom, B.S. et al. (1964), *Taxonomy of Educational Objectives: Affective Domain*, Longman, London.

Bloom, J. et al. (1988), "Students of the Open University of the Netherlands: developments 1984-88, The Open University of the Netherlands, Facts and Developments, OU/NL Centre for Education Technology Department for Research and Education, Aerleen, The Netherlands.

Brady, T.F. (1976), "Learner-Instructor Interaction in Independent Study Programmes", University of Wisconsin, Doctoral Thesis, Madison,

Brindley, J.E. (1987), *Attirition and Completion in Distance Education: The Studies Perspective*, Vancour: University of British Columbia.

Buch, M.B. (1979), *Second Survey of Research in Education, (1972-78)*, Society for Educational Research and Development, Baroda.

Cengiz et.al. (1989), "A Short Profile of the first Graduate of the Open Education Faculty" Anadolu University, Turkey, *ICDE Bulletin*, January, Vol.19.

Chakrabarthy, S. (1992), "A Comparitive Study of the attitude of traditional and Correspondence Students towards Distance Education", Unpublished M.Ed., Dissertation, Utkal University, Orisa.

Chander Jose. N. (1991), *Management of Distance Education*, Streling Publishers Pvt. Ltd., New Delhi.

Chandrasekaran, A. (1994), "Staff Development in Distance Education", Kakatiya Journal of Distance Education, School of Distance Learning and Continuing Education, Kakatiya University, Warrangal, Jan-June, Vol.3, No.l.

Chandra, A. (1987), *Distance Education in Home Science*, Department of Home Science education and Extension, Faculty of Home Science, M.S. University, Baroda.

Chia Noel (1992), "The role of external library in distance education, epistolo didaktika", *The European Journal of Distance Education*, Association of European Correspondence Schools, London.

Child, G.B. (1963), "Supervised Correspondence Education at USAFI in Brandenburg Memorial Essay" - 1. Madision: University of Winconsion.

Clennell, S. (1991), *Students in Active Retirement*, Talis, No.l., Toulouse, France.

Cole, S. (1987), " Towards a new emphasis in monitoring Open learning". Vol. 2 (3).

Costa, J. (1991), "Life Long Learning Around the World" Talis, No. 1,Toulouse, France.

Crooks (1987), "Open Learning Systems", *Indian Journal of Open Learning*, January, Vol. 9.

Danial, J. (1989), "Commonwealth of Learning Opens", *ICDE Bulletin*, January, Vol.9.

Danial, J. (1991), "Distance Education and Developing Countries", The Open University of United Kingdom.

David Nicoll (1985), "Staff development in a Distance Teaching Institution", New Zealand, ICDE 13th World Conference, Australia.

Deshmuk, K.G. (1986), "Genesis and Growth of Distance Education", *University News*, New Delhi, Vol. XXXIV, No.42.

Deshpande, M. Prakash (1992), "Yashwantrao Chavan Maharashtra Open University and its Academic Programmes, *Indian Journal of Open Learning*, Vol. 1.

Developments in Distance Education in Asia (1993): *An Analysis of Five Case Studies UNESCO & ICDE.*

Dichanz, H. (1992), "On the attituse of Teacher towards media paradigms and interpretations as exemplified by the television for schools." *Education*, Vol. 45, Pub. Institute for Wisen Schaffidra, Zusammanatblit, Germany.

Distance Education in Asia and the Pacific (1986), Proceedings of the regional seminar on distance education held at Bangkok, Thailand, From November 26 to December 3, Manila.

Dodds, T. (1972), *Multi Media Approaches to Rural Education*, Cambridge: International Extension College.

Duke, Chris (1978), "Open Education in Australia", *Bulletin of the UNESCO Regional Office for Education in Asia and Oceanacia.*

Dutt, Rudder (1981), "The concept of Open University applicable to Indian conditions" Paper presented in the 15th Annual seminar and the General body meeting of IUACE held at Nagpur University.

Dutt Rudder (1983), "Planning and Development of Distance education in India", Paper presented at the Pune University at the Annual meating of IUACE, New Delhi.

Dutt Rudder (1993), "Open University Vs Distance Education Directories, Keynote address at the national seminar held on January 20-21, 1993 at the Department of Correspondence Courses, Patiala University, *Journal of Educational Planning and Administration* (NIEADA), Vol.VII, July, No.3.

Easthope Gary (1975), *Community Hierarchy and Open Education*, Routledge & Kegan Paul, London.

Education for All (1990), *Framework of Action to meet basic learning needs declaration of world conference on education for all*, 5-9, March, Jomitien, Thailand.

Erdos, R.F. (1967), *Teaching by Correspondence*, London, Longman.

Erdos, R.F. (1975), "Establishing an institution teaching by correspondence," Paris, UNESCO.

Eswara Redy, V. (1988), "Note of the Open University System with particular reference to correspondence course in the light of UGC policy grants", Osmania University, Hyderabad.

Fakes, J. (1973), *The Desirability and Feasibility of an Australian Open Type University*, Melbourne: University of Melbourne.

Ferguson John (1975), *Open University from Within London*, University of London.

Fishbein Martin (1967), *Reading in Attitude Theory and Measurement*, John Wiley & Sons, Inc. New York.

Freitals, K.S. et al. (1986), "Factors affecting student success at the National open University of Venezula," *Distance Education*, March, Vol.7, No. 1.

Ganor Margalit (1988), Assignment Construction in Distance education in developing Distance education, ed. David Stewart and John Daniel, OSLO: ICDE 14th World Conference papers.

Garg, S.C. et al. (2004), "Open and Distance Learning in India: IGNOU's Contribution to Indian Society," *University News*, 42(46), Nov. 15-21.

Garrison, D.R. (1989), *Understanding Distance Education: A Framework for the Future*, Pub. Routedge, London.

Clatter, R., et.al. (1971), Study by Correspondence as enquiry into correspondence study for examinations for degrees and other advanced qualifications, London, Longman.

Goode Williams, J. (1952), *Methods in Social Research*, McGraw-Hill Kogakusha Ltd, New Delhi.

Cooler, D.D. (1979), *Counselling the Distance Student: Fact or Fiction*, Open Campus, Geelonng, Winter, the Center for Educational Services, Deakin University.

Gordon, W. Allport (1967), "Attitudes", *Reading in Attitude Theory and Measurement*, (Ed.) Martin Fishbein John Wiley & Sons Inc., New Delhi.

Grugeon, D. (1973), *Teaching by Correspondence in the Open University*, Milton Keynes: The Open University.

Gupta, M.L. (1987), "A study of the Institute of Correspondence Studies, University of Rajasthan," *Journal of Higher Education*, Vol.12, Nos. 1-3.

Gupta, M.P. (1994), "Impact of Distance education in learners of D.D.E. course in Rajasthan," D.D.E. Project work, IGNOU, Rajesthan.

Gupta, S.K. (1988), "Finance of the Institute of Distance Education Vis-a-Vis cost constraints and cost effectiveness, *Journal of Educational Planning and*

Administration, Vol. 2, Nos. 3&4, Special Education on Distance Education, NIPEA, New Delhi.

Hakemulder, J. (1978), "UNECADE, some thoughts on Distance Education", Addis Ababa, United Nations (EGA).

Hall Jan, W. (1978), Open Education in Newzealand Bulletion of the UNESCO regional office for education in Asia Oceania.

Harris, W.J.A. et al. (1977), *A Hand Book of Distance Education: Manchester Monographs* 7, Department of Adult and Higher Education, Manchester, U.K.

Harry, K. (1982), "The Open University International Documentation Center on Distance Learning," *ICDE Bulletin,* May, Vol. 2.

Harthaway (1978), "A study of attitude towards correspondence study," ICCE, *Newsletter,* Oct. 1978, Vol.8, No.3.

Hawkridge, D. (1976), *Setting up the Open University,* Milton Keynes: The Open University, IET.

Haya Saad Rawaf, et al. (1992), "Distance Higher Education for women in Saudi Arabia—Present and Proposed." *An International Journal,* Vol. 13, No. 1, University of Southern Queenstand, Australia.

Hemlata Talesra (1986), "Distance Education Backward Classes and the New Social Order," *University News,* November 8.

Henerson, E, Marlene et al. (1987), *How to Measure Attitude,* Sage Publishers, California.

Holmberg, B. (1977), *Distance Education: A Survey and Bibliography,* Kogan Page, London.

Holmberg, B. (1981), *Status and Trends of Distance Education,* Kogan Page, London.

Holmberg, B. (1982), *Recent Research into Distance Education,* Femunivestat, Hagen.

Holmberg, B. (1989), *Theory and Practice of Distance Education,* Routledge, London.

Hommadi, A.H. (1990), Open University, *Indian Bibliographies Bureau,* Delhi.

Inayat Khan (1994), "Way two communication in Distance Education," *Kakatiya Journal of Distance Education,* Kakatiya University, Warangal, Vol.3, No. 1.

Indian Distance Education Association (IDEA). (1994), Report of first national conference on "Quality of Distance Education" 3-5, November, 1993.

Indira Gandhi National Open University (1991), *Brochure on Audio and Video Programmes,* Communication Division, New Delhi.

Information Base on Open Universities, Distance Education Institutes and Correspondence Courses Institutes. (2003), Indira Gandhi National Open University, New Delhi.

Indu Ghai (1992), A Study of the Attitude of Distance Learners Towards the Evaluation system in operation in Distance Education System, *IGNOU Project Report,* New Delhi.

Ingrid (1991), "Significance of Face-to-Face and independent learning in Distance Education—A study of Open University in Taiwan," Ph.D., Thesis, University of California, Los Angels.

International Workshop (1983), Counselling in Distance Education, September 20th-22nd, 1982, Cambridge, U.K., Manchester: Open University, North West Region.

Jayagopal, R, et al. (1991), Evaluation of Teaching-Learning

Situation of M.Ed., Correspondence Education of Madurai Kamaraj University.

Jayagopal, R. (1982), "Inservice Training for teaching through principles of Distance Teaching," Paper presented at XII ICDL at Vancour, British Columbia, Canada.

Jayagopal, R. (1984), "Distance Learning" Paper presented at the Seminar on Women Education in its various facts with a view to its Qualitative Improvement, Organised by the Quaid-E-Millet Govt. College, Chennai.

Jayagopal, R. (1984), "Perspective plan of the Institute of Distance (Correspondence) Education (1984-86), University of Madras, Chennai.

Jayagopal, R. (1984), "Using Mass Media for Formal and Non-Formal Education", Paper presented at the Annual Conference and Workshop on Distance Education, Sponsored by IUACE, and University of Poona.

Jayagopal, R. (1988), "Women in Distance Education Role of Media" Paper presented in the workshop on Women in Distance Education, Organised by the WIN, Department of Adult and Continuing Education, University of Madras.

Jayasankar, K. (1993), Presidential address: First National Conference on "Quality of Distance Education" at Kakatiya University.

Jaya Uppala (1994), "Structural arrangements and practices in Distance Education: A Voew Point, *Kakatiya Journal of Distance Education*, Ed. Murali Manohar, School of Distance Learning and Continuing Education, Kakatiya University, A.P., Vol.3, No. 1.

Johnson (1985), *Radio Conference and Distance Education*, ICDE Bulletin, May, Vol.8.

Kaye (1991), *Distance Teaching Models at University level, in Distance Teaching for higher and Adult Education*, Croom Helm, London , U.K.

Keegan, D. (1990), *Foundation of Distance Education* (2nd edition), Routledge, London.

Khan, I. (1989), Why students dropout from correspondence courses, In Khan, I(Ed.), *Teaching at a Distance.*

Khanka, S.S. (1994), Use of Multi-Media vis-a-vis Quality of Distance Education, , School of Distance Education, Kakatiya University, A.P., Vol.3, No. 1.

Kishore Kumar, R. (1994), "The Role of the Academic Counsellors and the need for the training them," *Kakatiya Journal of Distance Education*, Kakatiya University, A.P., Vol.3.

Kothari Commission (1960), *Report of the Education Commission*, Ministry of Education, Government of India, New Delhi.

Kothari, C.R. (1990), *Research Methodology, Methods and Techniques*, Wiley Eastern Ltd., New Delhi.

Koul, B.N., et al. (ed.) (1998), "Studies in Distance Education", Associaton of Indian Universities and IGNOU, New Delhi.

Koul (1993), "Staff Development for Distance Education", Paper presented at the COL Workshop held at CIEFL, Hydrabad, A.P.

Kulandaisamy, V.C. (1992), "Distance Education in Indian Context", *Indian Journal of Open Learning*, Vol. 1, NO.2, India.

Kulandaisamy, V.C. (1993), "Vice-Chancellor's Report-Fourth

Convocation of Indira Gandhi National Open University, New Delhi.

Laaser Wolfram (2002) "A Virtual University Environment: The German experience", published in Advancing Virtual University Education, No.l. University of Joensuu, Joensuu, Finland. Laaser Wolfram, "Platforms for a Virtual University System" published by SETRAD", Bharadhidasan University, Tiruchirapalli.

Lewis Roger (1980), *Counselling in Open Learning: A case study,* National Extension College, Cambridge, U.K.

Lewis Roger, et al. (1986), *What is Open Learning ?,* Council for Education Technology, London.

Lewis Roger (1986), *The Open Learning Hand Book* 2, How to help learners assess their progress, London, Council for Education Technology, London.

Lewis Roger (1994), *How to Tutor and Support Learners: Open Learning Guide,* 3, Council for Education Technology, London.

Mackenzie, M. (1976), Student Reaction to Tutor Comments on the TMA, Teaching at a Distance, No. 5.

Mani Gomathi (1983), *Evaluation of Distance Education,* Ph. D. Thesis, University of Madras Chennai.

Mani Gomathi (ed.). (1988), "Women in Distance Education: Issues & Prospects, WIN of ICDE", Ph.D., Thesis, University of Madras, Chennai.

Matheswaran, V.P. (1995), "A Study of Attitude of Distance Learners towards Open University Systems with special reference to IGNOU", Unpublished Ph.D. thesis, University of Madras, Chennai.

Matheswaran. V.P. (1998), "Attitudinal study of Open Learners hailing from IGNOU", *Recent Researches in Education and Psychology*, Chandigarh,Vol.3, No.I-II

Matheswaran, V.P. (2001), "Utilization of the Supporting Service Systems by IGNOU Learners" Published in the *Educational Review*, Bangalore, Vol.44, No. 1.

Menmuir, K. (1982), Educational Technology by Distance Learning, Media in Education and Development.

Michael W. Neil (ed). (1981), *Education of Adults at a Distance*, The Open University Press, London.

Mishra, K.N. (1992), "A study of the attitude of Distance Learners Towards Distance Mode of Education" , DDE Project report, IGNOU, New Delhi.

Mohanasundaram, K. (2004), *Online Evaluation: A Modern Trend, Teaching Strategies"*, APH Publishing corporation, New Delhi.

Mohanty Jagannath (1992), "Development of Distance Education" *Journal of Educational Planning and Administration*, July, Vol. VI, No. 3.

Moor, M. (1983), On the Theory of Independent Study, Distance Education: International Perspectives, Ed. By Sewart, Keegan and Homberg, Croom Helm, New York.

Moor, M. G. (1977), On a Theory of Independent Study, Zitt, Papers, 16, Hagen, Fern Universitat.

Murali Manohar, K. (1992), "Distance Education in India: Problems and Prospects," *Kakatiya Journal of Distance Education*, Kakatiya University, A.P., Vol.1., No.2.

Murugan, K. (1994), "The status and prospects of Counsellor Training: The IGNOU Experience," *Indian Journal of Open Learning*, Vol.3, No. 1, IGNOU, New Delhi.

Muthumanickam, A. (1991), "Study of Selected Rural Television forums with regard to knowledge and

Attitude levels, of the Adult Learners", Ph.D. thesis, University of Madras.

Nagarajan, N. (1990), "Human Resource Development through Multi-Media forums with specific and reference to Radio forums," Ph.D. thesis, University of Madras.

Narasimha Rao, P.V. (1994), Inaugural Address Speech at Dr. B.R. Ambedkar Open University, Hyderabad, A.P.

National Policy on Education (1986), Government of India, Ministry of Human Resource Development, Department of Education, New Delhi.

Neil, W. Michael (1981), *Education of Adults at a Distance,* Kogan Page in association with the Open University Press, London.

Nigel, Paine (1985), *"The Use of New Technologies in Open Learning"* Paper presented in the ICDE, 13th World Conference held at Melbourne.

Openheion, A.N. (1976), *Questionnaire Design and Attitude Measurement,* Heinemenn Educational Books Ltd, London.

Parmaji, S. (1984), *Distance Education,* Sterling Publishers Pvt. Ltd., New Delhi.

Parthasarathy, K. (1987), "A study of Persuasive Communication Techniques and its effects on Adult Learning at selected Villages of Chingleput District in Tamil Nadu" Ph.D., thesis, University of Madras.

Paul, M. (1993), "The Development of an Instrument to measure student attitude towards televised courses", *The American Journal of Distance Education,* Vol. 7, No. 1.,The Pensylvania State University, U.S.A.

Penalvar, L.M. (1990), *Distance Education a Strategy for Development*: Key note Address-UNESCO, Venezuela.

Peters, Otto (1992), *Some Observations on Dropping Out in Distance Education.*

Pillai, J.K. (1984), Impact and Performance of Correspondence Education Programme of Madurai Kamaraj University, Department of Education, Madurai Kamaraj University.

Ponnam, K. Ashok (1992), A study on the effective of counseling in IGNOU: A case of D.D.E. Programme in Orissa.

Power, K.B. (2002) "Online education: The Quality Imperative", *University News*, January 28-February 03, Vol. 40., No. 4, New Delhi.

Prasad, V.S. (1994), "Staff training for Distance Education System: Some Issues," *Indian Journal of Open University*, Vol. 3, No. l, IGNOU, New Delhi.

Race, Phil. (1989), *The Open Learning Hand Book I:* Selection Designing and Supporting Open Learning Materials, Kogan Page, London.

Ralph Cable. (1968), *Audio Visual Hand Book*, University of London, U.K.

Ramalinggam, P.V. (1992), "Print Materials in Distance Education: Its importance and need for use of computers for production of good quality print materials, D.D.E., Project Report, IGNOU, New Delhi.

Ram Reddy, G. (1983), The Indira Gandhi National Open University: Its Role in Higher Education: Experience of Open Universities,20-22, November, New Delhi.

Ram Reddy, G. (1987), *Planning Management and Monitoring of Distance Education*, Vol. I, Manila, Asia Development Bank.

Ram Reddy, G. (1988), *Open Universities: The Ivory Tower Thrown Open*, Streling Publishers, New Delhi.

Rana Sudarsana (1994), *Open Learning in India,* Commonwealth Publishers, New Delhi.

Rana, T.G. (1986), "A Study of Attitude of Students of M.S. University towards Distance Education," Unpublished M.Ed., Dissertation, M.S. University, Baroda.

Rathore, H.C.S. (1993), *Management of Distance Education in India,* Ashish Publishers, New Delhi.

Reddy, K.V. (1992), "Mass Media in Education", *University News,* Vol. XXX, No.l.

Reddy, O.S. (1986), "Ingredients for the Success of Open Universities," *The Hindu,* 26th August, Chennai.

Rekkedel, T. (1983), "Research and Development Activities in the field of Distance Study at NK1 in Distance Education: International Perspectives, Ed. David Sewart, Desmond Keegan and Homberg, Croom Helm, London.

Rekkedel, T. (1985), Introducing the Personal .Tutor/ Counsellor in the System of Distance Education," Stebekk, Norway, NKI, Skohen.

Rekkedel, T. (1986), "The Tutor-Counsellor in Norway", *Journal of Open Learning,* February, Vol.1, No.l.

Rensis Likert (1967), The Method of Constructing an Attitude Scale: Reading in Attitude theory and Measurement (Ed.) Martin Fishbein, John Wiley & Sons, Inc. New Delhi.

Report of Workshop on Instructional Material (1978), September 20-22, 1978, Directorate of Correspondence Courses, Panjab University, Chandigargh.

Richard, (1989) "Staff Attitude towards Distance Education at the University of Zambia", *Journal of Distance Education,* Vol.4, No. 2, Canadian Association for Distance Education, Canada.

Roger, Levis (1984), *Open Learning in Action*, Council for Educational Technology, London.

Ronnie, Carr (1984), "Tailand's Open University", *ICDE Bulletin*, May, Vol.5.

Rudestam kjell Erik, et al. (2002), "Handbook of Online Learning" Innovations in Higher Education and Corporate Training, Published by Sage Publications, California.

Rumble, et al., (1982), *The Distance Teaching Universities*, Croom Helm Ltd., London.

Sahoo, P.K. (1985), "A Study of Correspondence Education in Indian Universities," Ph.D., Thesis, M.S. University, Baroda.

Sahoo and Bhatt, V.D. (1987), "A Study of Attitude of Students Towards Correspondence Education," *Journal of Indian Education*.

Sahoo, P.K. (1988), "Distance Education in the Himachal Pradesh University, A Case Study," *Journal of Education and Planning and Administration*, Vol. 2, NIEPA, New Delhi.

Sathyanarayana, P. (1992), *Distance Education: What? Why? And How?* Hyderabad, IGNOU Regional Centre.

Sathyanarayana, P. et al. (1992), "Student Assignments for submission in Distance Education," *Kakatiya Journal of Distance Learning and Continuing Education*, Kakatiya University, A.P.

Saraswathi Balasubramaniyam (1986), "The Status of Correspondence Courses in India" *University News*, November,8, Vol.XXIV, No.42, Special Issue, New Delhi.

Sewert David (1990), Preface in Marian Croft etc., (ed.) *Distance*

Education: Development and Access, International Council for Distance Education, Caracus.

Singh Bakshish (1989), " Distance Teaching - Learning System in India", *Journal of Distance Education*, Jammu, March, Vol. 1, No, 1.

Singh Bakshish, et al. (1992), "Correspondence and Distance Education in India: An indepth study, *The Research Project Report* (unpublished), New Delhi.

Singh Bakshish, et al. (1994), "Mechanism of Maintenance of Standards in Distance Education," *Kakatiya Journal of Distance Education*, Kakatiya University, A.P, Jan-June, Vol.3, No. 1.

Singh Bakshish, et al. (1994), Presidential address on "Increasing access to Distance Education: An Agenda for Action," *Open Ideas*, Vol.1, No.2, A.P.

Singh Bakshish (1988), "Student Support Services" in *Studies in Distance Education*, (ed.) B.N.Koul et al., Association of Indian Universities and IGNOU, New Delhi.

Sohanvir, Chaudry (1988), "Distance Education through Television experience from the community viewing Scheme," *New Frontiers in Education*, July-Sep, Vol. XVIII, No.3.

Solomon, G. (1985), "Using Television as Unique Teaching Research for Open University Courses, Milton Keys, The Open University, ICDE Bulletin, Vol.3.

Stinehart Kathleen Anne. (1987), "Factors affecting Faculty Attitude Towards Distance Teaching" IOWA State University.

Subramani (1977) "Growth and Development of Distance Education in Tamil Nadu - A Historical Study", Ph.D. thesis University of Madras.

Sudha Rao, K. (1988), "Open Learning System, Concept and Future," *Journal of Planning and Administration,* Vol.2, No.3&4, Special Education on Distance Education, NIPEA, Delhi.

Sudha Rao, K. (Ed.) (1989), *Open Learning System,* Lancer International, New Delhi.

Swaminathan (1994), "Increasing access to Distance Education: An agenda for action". *Open Ideas,* Vol.1, No.2, Warangal, A.P.

Takwala, R. (1988), "Dimensions and Extensions of Distance and Open Educational Systems," Book on *Studies in Distance Education,* Association of Indian Universities and IGNOU, New Delhi.

Taylor, H. (1969), *Students without Teachers the Crisis in the University,* New York.

Thampson, G. (1990), "A Survey of Attitude of Students who are not well disposed towards correspondence study", *Journal of Distance Education,* Vol. 1, No. 1, Canadian Association for Distance Education, Canada.

Thrustone, L.L. (1969), The Measurement of Social Attitudes, *Reading in Attitude Theory and Measurement* (ed.) Martin Fisbein, John Wiley & Sons, Inc, New York.

Tight Malcom (1988), " Open Learning and Continuing Education", Jarvins, P., (Ed.) *Policy and Practice in Continuing Education,* New Directions for Continuing Education, No.40, San Francisco; Jossey-Bass, winter.

Treitals, K.S. et al. (1986), "Factors affecting students success at the national Open University of Venezula", *Distance Education,* March, Vol.7, No.l.

Vice-Chancellor's Report (1993), Fourth Convocation, 4th May, Indira Gandhi National Open University, New Delhi.

Villi, C. (1993), "Study of Women Learners who had dropped out of the Open University System of the University of Madras," Ph.D thesis, University of Madras, Chennai.

Warren E. Hathaway (1978), "A Study of Attitude Towards Correspondence Study" *ICCE News Letter*, Vol.8, Oct. 1978.

Wedmeyer, et al. (1956) "Completion of University Correspondence Courses by Adults", *Journal of Higher Education.*

Ziqerell James (1984), *Distance Education in Information Age Approach to Adult Education.*

Appendix

Questionnaire

Please tick (✓) wherever applicable

Name of the Respondent :

Name of the Study Centre :

Programme : Certificate/Diploma
Under Graduate/Post Graduate

I. Socioeconomic Status of the Respondent

1.	Sex	:	Male/Female
2.	Age	:	
3.	Religion	:	Hindu/Muslim/Christian Others
4.	Community	:	SC/ST/MBC/BC/FC
5.	Residence	:	Rural/Urban
6.	Educational Background (at the time of joining the course)	:	Respondent/Parents/Spouse
7.	Occupation		
8.	Marital Status	:	Married/Unmarried/Others
9.	Type of Family	:	Nuclear Family/Joint Family
10.	Total Monthly Income	:	Rs.

II. Level of Utilising the Supporting Service System

1. When did you receive all the Self-Instructional Materials supplied by IGNOU?

a. Immediately after joining the course

b. Some time in the middle of the course

c. At the end of the course

2. What is the frequency of viewing IGNOU Television Programme?

   a. Regularly b. Often c. Rarely d. Not at all

3. What is the frequency of visiting to the study center library?

   a. Regularly b. Often c. Rarely d. Not at all

4. What is the frequency of attendance at the counselling?

   a. Regularly b. Often c. Rarely d. Not at all

III.	**Attitude to Admission Procedures**	S.A.	A.	U.D.	D.A	S.D.A.
1.	Any literate may be admitted in the Open University Systems					
2.	For joining Open University Systems there should be age restriction					
3.	The Open University Systems enables many to continue their education					
4.	Admission into the Open University Systems helps to save time					
5.	Open University Systems reaches all sections of the country					
6.	To join directly into the degree course, credit system is essential					
7.	Mother tongue should be the medium of instruction even at the degree level					
8.	Study through regular course and Open University Systems should be considered equally for jobs					
9.	Employed persons should join the Open University System for further promotion.					
10.	Learners join Open University Systems for improving knowledge.					

IV.	**Attitude to Self-Instructional Material (S.I.M.)**	**S.A.**	**A.**	**U.D.**	**D.A**	**S.D.A.**
1.	Self-Instructional Material have clear explanation.					
2.	The charts and illustrations provided in the S.I.M. are sufficient					
3.	S.I.M. are easy to read and understandable					
4.	S.I.M. mailed by the institution reach me in the specified time					
5.	It is enough to read S.I.M. for study purposes.					
6.	The details of all the required references are available in the S.I.M.					
7.	S.I.M. are printed without errors					
8.	S.I.M. inspire the learners to learn					
9.	Self-Instructional Material are informative					
10.	S.I.M. are based on the requirements of the learners					

V.	Attitude to IGNOU Television Programmes	S.A.	A.	U.D.	D.A	S.D.A.
1.	Television helps to take IGNOU programs to all the learners					
2.	Learners will get more benefit if IGNOU programs are broadcast over radio also					
3.	It is enough to telecast IGNOU programs three days a week					
4.	Telecasting time IGNOU program is suitable for learners					
5.	The total time of telecast is enough for the learners to understand the lessons					
6.	The telecast of IGNOU programmes are related to the syllabus Self-Instructional Material of the subject concerned					
7.	The IGNOU telecast programs are clear and easy to understand					
8.	The demonstrations of IGNOU program are motivating and interesting					
9.	Repeated explanations are given for difficult unit while telecasting by television program					
10.	Programs should be telecast/ broadcast in regional languages					

VI.	Attitude to Study Centre/ Library Facilities	S.A.	A.	U.D.	D.A	S.D.A.
1.	Study center cater to the needs of the learners					
2.	The number of study centers is sufficient					
3.	The study centers provide required explanations related to syllabus					
4.	Study centres located in educational institutions are preferable					
5.	It is convenient to have present timings for the study center					
6.	All related books are available in the Library					
7.	Audio-Video equipments are available for the learners in the Library					
8.	The atmosphere of Library is conducive to study					
9.	It is desirable to lend audio/video cassettes and books					
10.	It is desirable to keep open the library on all days					

VII.	**Attitude to Counselleors/ Counselling Services**	S.A.	A.	U.D.	D.A	S.D.A.
1.	It is desirable that the learners take part in the counselling session					
2	Counselling helps the learners to get their doubts clarified					
3.	Counselling timings are suitable to the learners					
4.	Counselling takes place at regular intervals					
5.	The number of Counsollers is sufficient					
6.	Experienced and subject experts handle counseling session					
7.	The techniques employed for Counselling are very good					
8.	The Counsellors need more exposure/experience in distance education					
9.	The counselors should understand the problems of distance learners and help them accordingly					
10.	Effective teaching aids are used in the counseling sessions					

VIII	Attitude to Evaluation: Assignment/Examinations	S.A.	A.	U.D.	D.A	S.D.A.
1.	Entrance Examination is essential for Open University Systems					
2.	Regular assignments is essential for evaluating the progress of the learners					
3.	After evaluation of assignments it should be returned to the learners within the time					
4.	Assignment motivates the learners					
5.	Writing assignments help the learners for prepare their examinations					
6.	Tutor comments also help to identify the strong and weak points of the learners					
7.	Project work at the higher level of studies is essential for imparting the research skills					
8.	The examination system twice a year is convenient for the learners					
9.	The time available for the preparation of the examinations is more than sufficient					
10.	There is great relevance between the materials supplied and the questions asked					

Index

❑❑❑